Simple
Sermons
about
Jesus
Christ

THE "SIMPLE SERMON" SERIES BY W. HERSCHEL FORD . . .

Seven Simple Sermons on the Saviour's Last Words
Seven Simple Sermons on the Second Coming
Simple Sermons About Jesus Christ
Simple Sermons for a Sinful Age
Simple Sermons for Funeral Services
Simple Sermons for Midweek Services
Simple Sermons for Saints and Sinners
Simple Sermons for Special Days and Occasions
Simple Sermons for Sunday Evening
Simple Sermons for Sunday Morning
Simple Sermons for Time and Eternity
Simple Sermons for Times Like These
Simple Sermons for Today's World
Simple Sermons for 20th Century Christians
Simple Sermons on Conversion and Commitment
Simple Sermons From the Book of Acts
Simple Sermons From the Gospel of John
Simple Sermons From the Gospel of Matthew
Simple Sermons on Evangelistic Themes
Simple Sermons on Heaven, Hell and Judgment
Simple Sermons on Prayer
Simple Sermons on Prophetic Themes
Simple Sermons on Salvation and Service
Simple Sermons on Simple Themes
Simple Sermons on the Christian Life
Simple Sermons on Great Christian Doctrines
Simple Sermons on the Old-Time Religion
Simple Sermons on the Seven Churches of Revelation
Simple Sermons on the Ten Commandments
Simple Talks for Christian Workers
Simple Sermons on Life and Living
Simple Sermons for Modern Man
Simple Sermons on Old Testament Texts
Simple Sermons on New Testament Texts
Simple Sermons for a World in Crisis
Simple Sermons on Grace and Glory

Simple Sermons about Jesus Christ

by
W. HERSCHEL FORD, B.A., D.D.

OF THE ZONDERVAN CORPORATION
GRAND RAPIDS, MICHIGAN 49506

SIMPLE SERMONS ABOUT JESUS CHRIST
Copyright 1961 by
Zondervan Publishing House
Grand Rapids, Michigan

Eighteenth printing 1980
ISBN 0-310-24491-9

Printed in the United States of America

DEDICATION
This book is affectionately dedicated to
Dr. and Mrs. Vaughn M. Johnson
of St. Petersburg, Florida,
two wonderful and devoted friends
who have meant much to me over the years.

PREFACE

Because of the splendid response given to my other books of *Simple Sermons*, I am happy to present this new volume entitled, *Simple Sermons About Jesus Christ*. I believe that we are preaching the Gospel in its highest form when we center our messages around the Saviour. I have tried to do that in these sermons.

I hope that these *Simple Sermons* will be a great blessing to many people, especially to my preacher brethren. They are perfectly welcome to use all of these messages in any way that would bring glory to God and souls to the Saviour.

W. HERSCHEL FORD

FOREWORD

Once again we are indebted to Dr. W. Herschel Ford for another in the "Simple Sermons" Series. This euphonic phrase has become synonymous with warm-hearted preaching of the highest caliber. The author is a master at expressing sublime truth in simple language, and that is preaching at its best.

This volume is exactly what it claims to be. It is *Simple Sermons About Jesus Christ*. It exalts Him as Lord. It presents Him as the eternal Christ who became flesh. It declares the age-abiding redemptive purpose of God in Christ, a purpose which was realized within the context of history. It relates this purpose to the needs of our day.

The author is the beloved pastor of one of America's great churches. His worth as a Kingdom leader has been recognized by his brethren who recently elected him as the Second Vice-President of the Southern Baptist Convention. Both personally and through his pen he renders a ministry of worldwide scope.

It just happens that the author and I have the same given name. Recently I received a letter asking me to send the writer a book of my "simple sermons." I replied that all my sermons are "simple," but that I was reasonably certain that he had in mind the sermons of my good friend, Dr. W. Herschel Ford. I referred him to this author. I would do the same for you. For a beneficial and delightful experience I refer you to *Simple Sermons About Jesus Christ*. You will not be disappointed.

HERSCHEL H. HOBBS

CONTENTS

1. The Seven Wonders of Jesus Christ — 15
2. The Greatest Visit Ever Made — 23
3. The Pre-Eminence of Christ — 29
4. The Cross of Christ — 37
5. The Greatest Man Alive Today — 47
6. The Gospel of Christ — 54
7. Have You Seen Jesus Lately? — 62
8. The Hope of the World — 69
9. Christ and the Home — 76
10. The Teachings of Christ Applied to Modern Life (Part One) — 83
11. The Teachings of Christ Applied to Modern Life (Part Two) — 90
12. If Jesus Came Back Tomorrow — 97

Simple Sermons about Jesus Christ

Sermon 1

THE SEVEN WONDERS OF JESUS CHRIST

Isaiah 9:6-7

In a small Italian town in the Alps there nestles a little church which is very unusual. Along the walls of the inside of the church there are several statues of Old Testament prophets. Each one faces the same way and the index finger of each prophet points in the same direction. As you follow the gaze of these prophets you will see that they are all looking at and pointing toward a larger statue of Jesus Christ. These statues are simply saying, "All of the Old Testament prophets point to Jesus. All of them strain their eyes in eagerness toward Calvary."

Now the prophet who spoke most of Jesus was Isaiah. He is the one who spoke of His birth when he said that a virgin would conceive and bring forth a child. He is the one who spoke of His death when he said, "He was wounded for our transgressions, he was bruised for our iniquities: the chastisement of our peace was upon him; and with his stripes we are healed." And in mighty and marvelous and descriptive language in the ninth chapter of his book, Isaiah uses one word to describe Jesus. He says, "He shall be called WONDERFUL." Now I am afraid that today we use this word to excess. We speak of a wonderful picture, a wonderful book, a wonderful song, a wonderful view. We speak of a wonderful baby, a wonderful boy or girl, a wonderful man or woman. Yet this word is totally inadequate in describing Christ. We could talk for hours of His wonders and then we would have to throw up our hands and say, "The half has never yet been told."

But today, as far as human speech can serve me, I want to tell you about the Seven Wonders of Jesus Christ.

I. THE WONDER OF HIS BIRTH

When the fulness of time came, when the clock of eternity struck the hour, God said, "It is time for My Son to leave the glory of heaven and go down into the world to redeem men from their sin." And how should He send Him? Should He send

Him as an angel? Should He send Him as a mighty King? Should He send Him as a full-grown man? No, none of these. He decides to send Him as a tiny babe and to let Him grow up in a normal way to manhood, that He might know all of the desires and all of the trials and all of the temptations of a normal man.

So God looks about to find a good woman to be the vehicle to bring His Son to birth. And His eyes lighted upon Mary, a devoted and dedicated young woman, pure in heart and lovely in life. Now God calls Gabriel to His side. "Go down," said He, "to Mary and tell her that she is going to have a child and that He will be called the Son of God. And when she asks how this can be, since she has had no relationship with a man, tell her that the Holy Spirit will bring all of this to pass." And Gabriel flexes his wings to fly away upon his errand. Then God says, "Gabriel, tell her that His Name shall be called Jesus." The message is given, both to Mary and to Joseph, whom she is soon to marry. And they accept the responsibility as becomes two fine and godly people. Then when the time arrives they journey to Bethlehem. And that starry night, while the angelic chorus sang, "GLORY TO GOD IN THE HIGHEST," the Son of God came into the world.

Oh, how wonderful was the virgin birth. Since Adam and Eve came into the world, no child has ever been born except through the fusion of a man's nature with a woman's nature. But no man had anything to do with the birth of Jesus. God Himself was the Father and Mary was the mother. Up in heaven He rested upon the Father's bosom without a mother, and in Bethlehem's stable He rested upon the mother's bosom without a father.

A few years ago a controversy arose in New York City and it was published across the country. A noted preacher said that he didn't believe in the virgin birth. Many people today feel the same way. But God says that He was born of a virgin, the angel Gabriel believed it, Mary and Joseph knew it, and the men who wrote the New Testament wrote about it. The whole Christmas story becomes alive when we see the baby Jesus lying in a manger and when we remember that He was God's own Son, whom He sent down into the world in a miraculous manner. Mary was just the vessel which He used to accomplish His purpose.

Has there ever been a birth like that of Jesus? No, never. He was wonderful in His birth.

II. THE WONDER OF HIS LIFE

There are several things in the New Testament which describe His life. First, He never committed a single sin. Peter says, "He did no sin, neither was guile found in his mouth." The writer of Hebrews says, "He was in all points tempted like as we are, yet without sin."

There have been some good men in the world, but only one perfect man. Jesus was that Man. No one could point to one bad thing in His life. Call Him before you today. Examine Him from every standpoint. Did He ever say an evil word? No. Did He ever do a wrong thing? No. Did He ever have a sinful thought? No. We must say with Pilate of old, "I find no fault in this just man."

A colored preacher announced that he was going to have a funeral service in his church at a certain hour. He did not announce the name of the deceased. The crowds came, the casket stood before the pulpit, and flowers were piled up on every side. The preacher did not eulogize the dead. Instead he said that the dead man had committed every known sin, that he was a wicked man and he would therefore go into eternal torment. When the sermon was ended, he invited the people to file past the casket to take a look at this horrible sinner. As the people looked they saw that the casket was empty except for a mirror that had been placed in it and every man and woman saw only himself. The preacher was simply saying that they were sinners. Ah, but look at Jesus. You can hold the microscope over His life, but you will find no sin in Him.

There may have been minutes when we didn't sin. There may have been hours when we didn't sin, but surely no day passes but that we sin in some way. But in all the minutes and hours and days and years that Jesus lived, there was no sin in Him.

Another thing about His life — He performed many marvelous miracles. He touched the blind and they were soon able to see. He touched the lame and they were able to walk. He cleansed the leper, stilled the storms and brought the dead back to life again. His life was simply filled with things which had never been done before or since, all because the power of heaven was His. There are scores of faith healers in the land today. They testify to the many miracles that they have performed. But I would like to say this — our hospitals and nursing homes are filled with suffering people. If these men can heal so easily, why don't they go to these hospitals and relieve the suffering of these thousands of sick people?

Another thing about His life was "that He went about doing good." Many people today go about, but they are not doing good. Jesus was goodness in action. Every mile that He traveled was full of the good things He was doing for someone else.

Albert Schweitzer, the missionary and scholar, was once scheduled to speak in an American city. A delegation of the most prominent men in the city met his train. When he got off the train these men rushed forward to greet him. They were going to make some speeches and take some pictures. As they neared him he said, "Excuse me, gentlemen." Then he went over to a little old lady, picked up her many bundles, carried them for her, and saw her safely into a cab. Then he came back to the amazed committee. We may not agree with all of Schweitzer's theology, but surely in this instance he was showing us a slight picture of Jesus, who went about doing good.

Another thing about Jesus' life was that He "spoke as never man had spoken before." I don't think that this means His eloquence and speaking ability so far exceeded that of others, but that what He said was so wonderful and so different.

He came and told men about a loving God. He told them how to make life worthwhile. He told them about a daily Companion who would help them in life and in death. He told them about the way of salvation. He told them about a glorious heaven awaiting the children of God. His discourses were not way off in outer space. He got down where men lived and touched them at the point of their greatest needs. Yes, Jesus was wonderful in His life.

III. The Wonder of His Death

He died as no other man ever died. Others have died sacrificial deaths, others have died for some great cause. But Jesus died to save men and bring them home to heaven. He didn't have to die. He said that He had power to lay down His life and power to take it up again. And He laid it down for you and me. "Greater love hath no man than this, that he give his life for his friends."

Do I need to remind you of that scene? Early in the morning they lay the cross upon Him and drive Him toward Golgotha. He faints beneath the load of the cross and Simon lifts it for

The Seven Wonders of Jesus Christ

Him. And when they come to the top of the hill, they lay the bruised and bloody body of the Saviour upon the cross. I can hear the ringing blows of the hammers as they nail great spikes through hands and feet. I can hear the dull thud as the cross is lowered into the hole prepared for it. For six long hours He hangs upon that cross, and even the sun in its sadness hides its face. Finally at three o'clock in the afternoon, after hours of anguish and intense suffering, He cries out, "It is finished!" and commends His spirit to God and dies.

But oh, look what He accomplished in His death. He opened up the fountain of cleansing from sin. He perfected salvation for every man. He flung open the gates of glory to every redeemed sinner. He opened the way whereby any man could find the pathway from sin to God.

A minister was boarding for a time in a farmhouse. The farmer was not a Christian, but his wife had been praying for him for a long time. The preacher was just waiting to make plain to him the meaning of Christ's death on the cross. One morning the farmer asked the preacher to go out with him to the chicken house. There on a nest sat a hen with her brood of chickens peeping out from under her wings. The farmer told the preacher to touch the hen, but when he did so he found that she was dead. The farmer said, "Look at the wound in her head. A weasel has sucked out all the blood from her body, but she never once moved for fear that the little beast would get her chickens." Then the preacher said, "Oh, that is just like Christ! He endured all that suffering on the cross. He could have moved and saved His own life, but if He had moved, you and I would have been lost." The farmer saw the point and soon accepted Christ as his Saviour.

And He did all of this for you and me. If we had been the only lost persons on earth, He would have done this for us. Now I would like to ask you a pointed question. "Since Christ did all of this for you, what are you doing to make it up to Him? What are you doing for the One who loved you and gave Himself for you?" He says:

> I gave My life for thee,
> My precious blood I shed,
> That thou mightst ransomed be,
> And quickened from the dead.
> I gave, I gave My life for thee,
> What hast thou given for Me?

IV. The Wonder of His Resurrection

Yes, they slew Jesus and buried Him, but no tomb on earth could hold Him. On the third day, just as He prophesied that He would, He walked out of that tomb, alive forevermore. The Resurrection proves that He was the Son of God; it proves that everything He ever said was true. The Resurrection set a seal upon His divinity. Dr. Harry Rimmer was talking to a high official in the Egyptian government, who was a Moslem. Dr. Rimmer said, "We believe that God revealed Himself to man." And the Moslem answered, "We believe that, too." Dr. Rimmer said, "We believe that God revealed Himself in creation." And the Moslem answered, "We believe that, too." Dr. Rimmer said, "We believe that God revealed Himself in a book, the Bible." The Moslem answered, "We believe that God revealed Himself in a book, the Koran." Dr. Rimmer said, "We believe that God revealed Himself in a man, Jesus Christ." The Moslem said, "We believe that God revealed Himself in a man, the prophet Mohammed." Dr. Rimmer said, "We believe that Jesus died to save His followers." The Moslem said, "We believe that Mohammed died for his people." Dr. Rimmer said, "We believe that Jesus was able to substantiate all of His claims because He rose from the dead." Then the Moslem answered, "We have no information concerning our prophet after death." Yes, Jesus Christ is supreme because He is the only One who ever conquered death and triumphed over the grave.

The difference in Christianity and every other religion is that their founders are dead. Ours rose from the grave and is alive again. At the tombs of Mohammed and Confucius and Buddha and all the others, we read, "Here he lies." But when we go to the tomb of Jesus, the words of the angel ring out upon our ears, "He is not here, He is risen." Yes, He was wonderful in His resurrection.

V. The Wonder of His Ascension

In the spring of 1961 a man was lifted into space. All the world stood agog at this achievement of human science. But this was not the first time there has been a man in space. After spending forty days on the earth following His resurrection, Jesus led His disciples out to the Mount of Olives. And there, while they looked on in open-mouthed amazement, Jesus went up to heaven in a cloud. He didn't have a launching pad nor booster rocket, nor space suit, nor a helmet, nor one piece of electronic equipment. He had just one ordinary cloud, but up He went, back to heaven, back to God the Father, back to the glory that He had before the world began. What a homecoming that must have been! The angels sang their sweetest songs, the saints shouted and rejoiced, and once more God clasped His only begotten Son.

Look at the importance of the ascension. In His resurrection Jesus was marked out to be the Son of God in power. In His ascension He was marked out as Lord. In His resurrection is shown His power over death. In His ascension He is shown to have all power in heaven and in earth. Death is shown to be subject to Him in the Resurrection. All things are shown to be subject to Him in His ascension. We read that "God hath highly exalted him, and given him a name that is above every name." This happened when He ascended into heaven. Since His ascension He holds the central place in glory. He said, "It is expedient for you that I go away. Then the Holy Spirit will come to do His mighty work in hearts all over the world." So Jesus goes home to God and glory, and soon the Holy Spirit comes down to take His place upon the earth.

VI. The Wonder of His Present Work

What is Jesus doing in heaven today? He is carrying on the work of intercession. He is praying for us. "He ever liveth to make intercession for us."

Often I receive a letter from someone saying, "I am praying for you." I appreciate this, but let me tell you something finer. Up in heaven the Lord Jesus Christ has the ear of the Father and He intercedes for me from day to day. Dr. T. L. Holcombe, one of our elder ministers, recently announced that he was going to give the rest of his life to the ministry of intercessory prayer. And that is just what Jesus is doing for us up in heaven.

VII. The Wonder of His Coming Again

Back in the Old Testament days the prophets sang of His first coming. But the years passed and hope grew dim and people forgot the promise. Then when He came they knew Him not. They were not prepared for Him. In like manner the Bible tells us that He is coming again. But the years have gone by and many have said, "Where is the sign of His coming?" And since He hasn't come yet, they let the promise slide into oblivion. But just as surely as He came the first time, He must come the second time. The prophecies must be fulfilled. They are not vain promises. They are the sure Word of an Almighty God.

When He comes, He will come to bless. Oh, how we need His blessing today! When He comes in the air, the Bible tells us that He is going to take all believers up to heaven. He is going to change them into His own glorious likeness. Then, oh what a blessed promise, we read, "So shall we ever be with the Lord." This will be the first phase of His coming — His coming for us.

Later He will gather all of His saints around Him in heaven and come back to the earth with them. This old world is in a mess now. Then He will straighten things out and reign upon the earth in righteousness for a thousand years. Thus saith the Scriptures. Thus do I believe.

He will also come to judge. When He takes the Christians up in the air He will judge their works and reward them accordingly. The trouble with many Christians is that they are doing nothing for the Lord. They will have no works to be judged; there will be no reward for them. Later at the Great White Throne He will judge the works of unbelievers and punish them according to their works. Oh, sinner, come to Jesus so that you can escape that judgment!

These are the seven wonders of Christ. There are a million more connected with all of these events. When we have been in heaven ten thousand years we will still not be able to count up all the wonders of this wonderful Saviour.

A certain family was having a "family reunion." The grandparents were there, the children were there, many grandchildren were there. The long tables were filled with food. Sweet fellowship abounded. Everybody was having a good time. Then one of the little boys went over to his grandmother's side. He looked up and saw tears on her cheeks. He couldn't understand it. She ought to have been happy with all of her loved ones around her. So he said, "Grandmother, what is the matter? Why are you crying?" And she answered, "Because it just occurred to me that this may be the last time I will ever see them all together again in this world." Then she drew the little boy close and said, "But that's all right, for if I never see them again in this world, I know that I shall meet them in heaven, because every one of them is trusting the Lord Jesus Christ as Saviour."

How is it with you? How is it with your family? All the wonders of Christ will not avail for you if you don't come and accept His wonderful salvation.

Sermon 2

THE GREATEST VISIT EVER MADE

John 1:1-13

As we look back over the corridors of time we see that many wonderful visits have been made. In the early days of the world, when Adam and Eve were living in the Garden of Eden, God came down every evening and walked with them through that beautiful Garden. That was a wonderful visit. . . . Later on, when the world was sunk in sin, God came down and visited Noah. He told him that He was going to destroy the world with a flood and commanded him to build an ark to save the race. That was a wonderful visit. . . . Then came the day when God came to Abraham and commanded him to take his only son, Isaac, and offer him up as a sacrifice. God was simply testing Abraham's love. This was a wonderful visit. . . . After Paul met Christ on the Damascus road, after he heard the voice from heaven, he was led into the city where he prayed as a blind man for three days. Then God sent Ananias to tell him what God wanted him to do. Thus began the world's greatest gospel ministry. That was a wonderful visit. . . . On one of Paul's journeys he came to Miletus and called all the elders of Ephesus to meet him. Down by the seashore they had a great meeting. He charged them to be true to Christ and the Gospel and told them good-by. Then, knowing that they would never see their preacher again, they wept and kissed him farewell. That was a wonderful visit. . . . When John was an old man, he was banished to the Isle of Patmos for the crime of preaching the Gospel. There God pinned back the curtain of eternity, showed John what was to happen in the future, and told him to write it down in the Bible. That, also, was a wonderful visit.

But the most wonderful, the most glorious, the most meaningful visit ever made was when God became flesh and visited this world in the form of His Son. You know all the details of that virgin birth, that sinless life, that vicarious death, that victorious resurrection and ascension. John speaks of that visit and how Christ was received. There are four things which we see here in the text.

     I. The Creation
     II. The Coming
     III. The Crime
     IV. The Converts

I. The Creation

In verse 3 we are told that "all things were made by him; and without him was not anything made that was made." Who was John talking about? He was talking about the Lord Jesus Christ. We say that God created all things. Yes, He did, but He created through His Son. Verse 1 tells us that Jesus was in the beginning with God. Go back to the time when God created the world and you will find Jesus by His side. When God said, "Let there be light," Christ was there. When God said, "Let us make the seas and the dry land," Christ was there. When God said, "Let us make the animals and the fish and the fowl," Christ was there. When God said, "Let us make man in our own image," Christ was there as the agent of creation.

Now man doesn't create anything. He simply makes something out of existing material. But Christ as the agent of creation made everything out of nothing. He simply spoke and it came into being. A man can build a skyscraper a hundred stories high. He can build a bridge to span a mighty river. He can build a plane which flies six hundred miles per hour. He can build a ship which sails upon the water or a submarine which runs under the water. He can make vitamins which build men up or bombs which tear them down. But in all of his building, he must use material which is already here. Only God can create out of nothing.

Jesus created the blue heavens above. Jesus created the space between earth and sky. Jesus scooped out the rivers and lakes and oceans and filled them with water. Jesus put the sun and the moon and the stars where they are. Jesus put the flowers in the fields and the trees in the forests. Jesus put the fish in the sea, the birds in the air, and the animals on the land. Then Jesus made His masterpiece, man, and put him down here in the world.

As the song says, "The great Creator became our Saviour." God is the source of creation, but Jesus was the instrument bringing to pass all that we see in the world. So we look back and see that Jesus was living with the Father in the beginning, ages before that wonderful visit to earth.

II. THE COMING

There came a day in heaven when God decided to send His Son into the world. Why did He do that? There was only one reason. He saw men lost here and going to hell, and He wanted to provide a way of salvation. So God sent His Son into the world that the world through Him might be saved. He came as a babe, He grew up to manhood, He went about doing good, performing many miracles and teaching the great truths of God. Finally He was crucified upon Calvary's cross. And as He hangs there, we see God's purpose being fulfilled. Christ came not primarily as a doer of good deeds and a teacher of great truths. He came to die for sinners. *Romans 5:8* — "God commendeth his love toward us, in that, while we were yet sinners, Christ died for us."

Especially at Christmas time do we hear men telling why they think Jesus came into the world. Some say that He came to bring peace to the nations. If so, He has failed, because the world has not known universal peace. Some say that He came to set an example of brotherly love for us, teaching us to do kind things for others. Some say that He came to establish a brotherhood of man and a fatherhood of God upon the earth. Oh, why do men get so far away from God's Word? One verse is enough to tell us why He came. All of us know that verse, "God so loved the world that he gave his only begotten Son, that whosoever believeth in him should not perish, but have everlasting life." That's why He came.

The gold rush came to California in 1849. In 1850 a Methodist preacher arrived on the scene. He came not seeking gold but the souls of men. There was no church there where he could preach and no congregation interested in the things of God. But the people were there and he knew that they needed Christ. So on Sunday mornings he would stand upon a barrel and shout, "What's the news? What's the news?" Then when the crowd gathered around him he would say, "Thank God, I have good news for you, this morning, my brothers." Then he would tell them of Christ.

Oh, this world has received some good news over the centuries, but the greatest, grandest news ever received was the news that Christ was born, born to give the second birth, born to die that we might forever live.

Several years ago a young doctor went to China as a medical missionary. He was soon confronted with a disease which was killing off many people, but for which he knew no remedy. The disease was not listed in any medical book and there was no laboratory where he could do research work. So the young doctor did a daring thing. He studied patient after patient and filled his note book with a list of their symptoms. Then he filled some tubes with the germs of the disease and sailed for America. Just before he landed in New York he took these deadly germs into his own body, then hurried to Johns Hopkins hospital. He presented himself as a guinea pig to the doctors and professors there. They studied the disease and found a remedy. By the grace of God the young doctor lived and carried the remedy back to China, there to save hundreds of lives.

That is a slight picture of what the coming of Jesus meant. He saw men dying in their sin. And what did He do? He came and took our sin in His own body and died of the disease on the cross. That was the purpose of His coming. He came to die that we might forever live.

III. THE CRIME

Here it is in verse 11 — "He came unto his own, and his own received him not." This is earth's blackest sin. The rejection of the Lord Jesus Christ is the world's greatest crime. The men who start wars and bring sorrow and death upon millions of people are committing crime. The man who puts the bottle to his neighbor's lips commits crime, so says the Bible. The man who murders, who steals, who breaks the other laws of God is a criminal. But here is the greatest crime. Jesus came with His hands full of blessing, holding them out to the men of His day. But they rejected Him. They turned their backs upon Him. They finally killed Him.

As we think about these things today you may say, "I wouldn't have treated Him that way. I would have taken Him into my heart and home and given Him the best that I had." I wonder ... I wonder. He comes to men today even as He did then, but like the innkeeper, they have no room for Him. Yet we know who He is and what He can do for us, and those men of old didn't know these things. Surely our crime is greater than theirs.

Why don't men receive Jesus in their hearts? It is because

those hearts are too full of the things of this world. Why don't they take Him into their social lives? It is because He would "cramp their style." They want to do the things in social life that He would not approve of. Why don't they take Him into their business lives? Because then every deal would have to be as honest as the sunlight and they would not make as much money. Why don't they take Him into their home lives? Often it is because the family knows that their lives don't measure up and they would be hypocrites if they talked there about Jesus.

But why continue to be a criminal? Why not make a new start today? Why not make room in every area of life for Jesus? I read the other day of how one man went into another man's office and shot him several times, killing him in cold-blooded, pre-meditated murder. Then I said to myself, "How foolish is this man. Now he knows that he has no life left for himself. It's either the electric chair or life imprisonment for him." But the man who rejects Christ is the greater fool — He has nothing left for himself but death and hell.

IV. THE CONVERTS

Verse 12 says that "as many as received him, to them gave he the power to become the Sons of God." It is not as many as lived good lives, nor as many as joined the church, nor as many as were baptized, but as many as received Him. There is just one way to become a child of God. . . You must receive Jesus Christ as your personal Saviour.

There are many who admire Christ. There are many who believe that He is the Son of God. There are many who read about Him. There are many who love to hear songs and sermons about Him. But they have not received Him. And that's the one thing they must do to have eternal life. And the minute they receive Him in their hearts, they will want to confess Him before men. For the Bible says, "With the heart man believeth unto righteousness, and with the mouth confession is made unto salvation, for whosoever believeth on him shall not be ashamed."

And what do these become who receive Christ as their Saviour? They become the sons of God. And, oh, the marvelous things God will do for His children! He'll wash away their sins. He'll give them peace of heart and mind. He'll walk down life's pathway with them all the way. He'll be with them in the hour of death. He'll take them home to heaven at the close of life's day.

Dr. R. G. Lee won a young man and young woman to Christ. He baptized them and later married them. A year later a baby girl came to knit their hearts closer to each other and to God in love. Then one midnight the young man called and said, "Dr. Lee, we need you. Please come to the hospital. I'm afraid that our baby is dying." The preacher went to the hospital and found that the doctors and nurses were doing all that they could. But he and the parents had to stand by and watch the baby die. Dr. Lee tried to comfort the couple, but words seemed to be in vain. Soon the undertaker came, wrapped the baby in a little shawl, and started out with her. Then the young mother cried out, "Oh, let me have my baby just one more night. Please, just one more night." The husband turned and said, "Preacher, what must I do?" Dr. Lee replied, "Let her have the baby. Let her have it just one more night." The undertaker put the child, wrapped in the beautiful shawl, into the mother's arms. The preacher then went home with them. He said that the mother sat there all night with the little dead baby in her lap. She cooed and talked to the baby, but there was no light in the baby's eyes, no laughter on its lips, no warmth in the little body. Yet she had it — just one more night.

But for the children of God there is a Land where there is no night, no death, no sorrow. It is the land where we shall have our loved ones, not for just a little while, but forever and ever. I am so glad that Jesus visited the world and made all of this possible. I am glad that He went to Calvary for us all and I am glad that He can visit any open heart, bringing joy and peace and eternal life to that heart.

Sermon 3

THE PRE-EMINENCE OF CHRIST

Colossians 1:18

One Sunday after a morning service, a woman spoke to me and in a very gracious and warm manner she said, "Pastor, I never get tired of hearing you talk about Jesus." The true preacher never tires of talking about Jesus — the true Christian never tires of hearing about Him. So this morning, for a few minutes, let us turn our thoughts away from every plan and program and project and let us think about Jesus.

The text says that Christ should have the pre-eminence in all things. Sometime ago I stood on the top of Pike's Peak and looked down upon all the other mountains round about. Pike's Peak is the pre-eminent mountain in all of that mountainous region. . . . In the ancient city of Rome a golden milestone was set up in the center of the city. Every milestone in the great Roman Empire was measured out from this golden milestone. It was the pre-eminent milestone in all the Roman Empire. . . . The astronomers tell us that there is one fixed star in the heavens. They measure all the other stars by this fixed star. It is the pre-eminent star in all the solar system. . . . In Washington, D.C., all the downtown streets and avenues run toward the capitol. The capitol of our country is the pre-eminent building in the beautiful city of Washington.

And Jesus Christ is the greatest and the most pre-eminent Personality of all the ages. All of history past and all of prophecy future revolve around Him. He is above all others as a mountain is above a molehill, as the mighty ocean is above a drop of water, as the great sun is above a flickering candle, as a towering skyscraper is above a dollhouse. Let us see how Christ is pre-eminent.

I. CHRIST IS PRE-EMINENT WITH THE FATHER

We hear John say, "In the beginning was the Word, and the Word was with God, and the Word was God." We hear Jesus saying, "Before Abraham was, I am." Go back into the dateless past, before the world was formed or the morning stars sang together and there you find Jesus in the bosom of the Father.

Christ was with the Father in creation. "By Him were all things made, and without Him was not anything made that was made." Christ was with God when He said, "Let there be light." He was with God when He said, "Let us make a world." He was with God when He said, "Let us make man in our own image." Christ was there with God in all of eternity past. Project your mind just as far back as your imagination can carry you — back to the time when there was no world, before the moon and the stars and the sun were flung into space, when there was no sea, no land, no living creatures, no man. And standing there in the bright light of eternity past you will see God. But Christ was by His side. We say that Jesus was born nineteen centuries ago. That is true. "The Word became flesh and dwelt among us." But in reality, Christ existed with the Father in all of eternity past.

Now God has always made much of His Son. He has exalted Him above all the earth and given Him a Name that is above every name. If we want to please God, *we* must make much of His Son. When someone brags on one of our children, it pleases us greatly. How much more then is God pleased when we exalt His only begotten Son!

Today people say that they believe in God, but not in Christ. God despises such. The only way to God is through the Son. During the war we heard men say that they found God in a foxhole or on the deck of a ship. If they found Him, they found Him through Christ the Son, who said, "No man cometh unto the Father but by me."

God blesses the preacher who exalts Christ and tells of God's Son. He blesses all who love and follow His Son. Christ is preeminent with the Father — He has the first place in His heart and He ought to have the first place in our hearts. Robert Browning said, "Open my heart and you will see, engraved upon it, Italy." If your heart and mine are opend, one ought to find engraved thereon the matchless Name of Jesus Christ.

II. Christ Is Pre-Eminent in the Scriptures

The Bible story from beginning to end is the story of the Lord Jesus Christ. Now the Name of Jesus or Christ as such is not mentioned in the Old Testament. Yet He is the key to the Old Testament. You cannot understand the Old Testament un-

The Pre-Eminence of Christ

less you see that it points to Christ. The Old Testament is simply a sign-board saying, "This way to Jesus Christ."

The Old Testament is full of types and shadows which point to Christ. The brazen serpent on the pole points us to the One lifted up on the cross, saying, "Look unto me and be ye saved." The smitten rock points to the Rock of Ages cleft for us on Calvary — a place where we can go and hide from all of our sins. The manna from heaven reminds us of that One who became the bread of life for our hungry souls. The story of Abraham and Isaac reminds us of how God spared not His own Son, but gave Him up as a ransom for our sins.

Sometime ago I knew a young man who practiced the trade of a barber during the week and preached at a little country church on Sunday. A rich Jewish merchant, who was one of his customers, became interested in him and offered to teach him the Old Testament Scriptures. Every Sunday afternoon the young barber-preacher would go out to this man's house and was greatly helped by his study of the Old Testament. On a certain day their Bibles were opened to the 53rd chapter of Isaiah. The young man began to read the chapter and soon came to the words, "He was wounded for our transgressions, he was bruised for our iniquities; the chastisement of our peace was upon Him and by His stripes we are healed." Looking over at his teacher, the young man asked the question, "Who is the prophet speaking of here?" The Jewish merchant closed the Bible and said, "I do not know." And I say to you that the Old Testament is a closed Book if we do not see Jesus in it.

There is an old tradition about the building of Solomon's Temple. He sent into every country under the sun for his materials. In one shipment they found a queer-shaped piece of marble. There seemed to be no place for this marble, so it was rolled over into a ditch. Several years later the Temple was complete except for the keystone for the arch. They began to search for this keystone. A workman who had been there for many years said, "Some years ago a queer piece of marble was discarded here at the building site. Maybe that is the stone you are looking for." They finally found the stone, and when they put it in place, it fitted perfectly and the building was complete. Likewise Jesus is the Keystone of the Scriptures. Leave Him out of the Bible and it is a closed Book. Put Him in and everything fits perfectly and only then does it become the greatest of all Books.

III. Christ Is Pre-Eminent in Salvation

Men search everywhere for salvation, for forgiveness of sin, for hope of everlasting life. They try doing penance, they try good works, they try church membership, they try ritual, they try making large gifts to charity. But they find no peace, no assurance, and no hope in these things. A man never finds peace of heart until he realizes that "there is none other name given under heaven among men whereby we must be saved."

When George Nixon Briggs was governor of Massachusetts, three of his friends made a trip to the Holy Land. While there they climbed the hill of Calvary and cut a small stick from a bush. They made this stick into a walking cane. When they came back home, they went to the executive mansion and presented the cane to the governor. One of them said, "We wanted you to know that we thought of you when we climbed the hill of Calvary." The tears came into the governor's eyes and he said, "I want to thank you for thinking of me and for bringing me the cane, but I am more grateful that there was another One who thought of me when He climbed Calvary's Hill and shed His blood for my sins."

There are some things more valuable than silver and gold. The salvation we enjoy is worth more than all the world. "What shall it profit a man, if he shall gain the whole world, and lose his own soul?" Ask any Christian how much he would take for his hope in Christ. He may have grown cold, his interest may have waned, his mind may be filled with doubts, but he would answer, "I would not give up my hope in Christ for all the world." And yet all of this is free. "The gift of God is eternal life." Only heaven is ours for the asking.

And where does our salvation center? Not in creeds, nor in churches, not in our goodness nor our righteousness, but in a Man, Christ Jesus. He is "The Lamb of God which taketh away the sin of the world." He is pre-eminent in salvation. Our salvation begins and ends in Him. We are redeemed not by gold and silver, but by the precious blood of the slain Son of God.

IV. Christ Is Given Pre-Eminence by the Holy Spirit

Jesus said, "When he comes, he will testify of me." That is just what He does — all of His work is centered in Christ. First, He brings a man to see his sin, and a man can see that sin only against the dark background of Calvary. Then He points that

The Pre-Eminence of Christ

man to Christ as his only hope. In all the work of the Holy Spirit, Christ is given pre-eminence.

V. CHRIST SHOULD BE GIVEN PRE-EMINENCE IN ALL OUR CHURCH LIFE, WORK, AND WORSHIP

1. *He should be given pre-eminence in the prayers that are offered.* He said, "If ye shall ask anything in my name, I will do it." I wonder if any prayer is acceptable to God if it is not offered in the Name of Christ.

Sometimes one of our preachers joins a civic club. At the first meeting the president calls on him for a blessing. He offers a short prayer, using the Name of Christ. After the meeting the president says to him, "Preacher, we are glad to have you in our club, but there are some men in the club who do not believe in Christ. When you pray in the future, please don't use the Name of Christ in your prayer." Well, if that preacher has to deny his Lord in order to stay in that club, he had better get out of it.

I know a man who roomed in college with a fine young man whom we shall call Bill. One time Bill had to make his way across the state and since he had no money, he was forced to hitchhike. On the first night out he came to the home of his roommate's father and mother. He knocked on the door and the father came to the door, saying in a very gruff voice, "What do you want? " Bill said, "I know your son. He is my roommate in college." The father literally reached out and pulled the boy into the house, crying out, "Mother! Come here! Here is a boy who knows our son." That night the mother prepared a wonderful supper for the boy. After supper they sat around talking about the son who was away at school. When the bedtime hour came, Bill was given the best bed in the guest room. The next morning the mother prepared another fine meal for him. When the time came for Bill to leave, the father, who was noted for being tight and stingy, pulled out his pocketbook and gave the boy enough money to carry him to his destination.

Now why did this father do all of this for Bill? It was because this boy knew his son. So God says, "If you know My Son and ask anything in His Name, I will give you all that you need." Christ is to be pre-eminent in every prayer that is offered.

2. *Christ is to be pre-eminent in the songs that we sing.* We hear some very cheap songs today, but the songs that live and bless our lives and lift us up to God are the songs which were

written out of the deep heart experiences of men. We sing about Jesus the Lover of our souls. We sing about the Rock of Ages. We sing about Jesus keeping us near the cross. We sing, "All Hail the Power of Jesus' Name." The good songs are the ones which exalt Jesus Christ.

3. *Christ is to be pre-eminent in the sermons that are preached.* Paul said, "We preach Christ." Oh, we would wish today that a tide of real Gospel preaching could flow out from every pulpit in our land. We wish that every creature upon the face of the earth could hear the true Gospel of the Lord Jesus Christ. This is the only message that we have — it is the only message that we need. It is the only message that will bring results. Christ ought to be the center of every sermon.

4. *Christ is to be pre-eminent in the ordinances that are observed.* These ordinances were given to exalt Him. In baptism we are not to see the candidate, but we are to see the death, burial, and resurrection of Christ. In the Lord's Supper we are not to see the bread and the wine, but we are to look back toward a crucified Christ, and to look forward toward a coming King. Christ is to be pre-eminent in the ordinances.

5. *Christ is to be pre-eminent in the service that we render.* We have people who are faithful to a Sunday school class, faithful to a Training Union, to a W.M.U. Circle, or to the Brotherhood. But Christ is not pre-eminent with them, and they are not faithful to His Church. If something goes wrong in one of these organizations, they quit everything entirely. Christ is not given the pre-eminence in their service. We criticize the Catholics for putting ritual and form and the trappings of religion above Christ. But our people are just as guilty when they put the organizations of the church before Jesus Christ.

A great preacher who died sometime ago after a wonderful ministry, said just before his death, "It seems that all that I have ever done was done in the energy of the flesh." We often feel the same way ourselves, but when we make Christ pre-eminent and go forth in the power of the Holy Spirit, the heavens open up and the blessings come down.

The world will cast its flowers at our feet and honor us with its highest honors, but these are not the things that count. We must keep our eyes upon Jesus and give Him the pre-eminence in all the service that we render.

VI. Christ Will Be Pre-Eminent in the Great Prophetic Drama

I don't know all about the future as some claim to know, but I do know this Bible truth. I know that Jesus is coming back again someday. We can say with Job, "For I know that my redeemer liveth, and that He shall stand at the latter day upon the earth; and though after my skin worms destroy this body, yet in my flesh shall I see God; whom I shall see for myself, and mine eyes shall behold and not another."

When I was a boy my oldest brother went away to the city to work. We loved him very much and we missed him very much. About every six weeks he would come home for the weekend. A letter would arrive the first part of the week telling us that he was coming home. I knew what this meant. We would have our best meals, we would have some fine fellowship with my brother, and he would possibly give me some spending money. Well, on Saturday afternoon, I would get cleaned up and ready to meet him. It was a thrill to see him as he got off the train. We had a good time in our home and when I showed my school report card to him, he would reward me with a gift of money. Jesus Christ, my Elder Brother, has gone away. But He is coming back again someday. I want to be true to Him. I want to be busy for Him. And I want to have a good report to show Him when He comes.

I sat in a doctor's office in Jacksonville, Florida, and on the wall just behind him I saw a sign saying, "Perhaps Today." I knew what he meant. Perhaps Jesus may come back today — are you ready for His coming?

Judgment will take place when He comes. Every Christian shall stand before the Judgment Seat of Christ. Their works as a Christian will be judged and they will be rewarded accordingly. Later, every lost person will stand before the Great White Throne Judgment. They will be judged according to the deeds done in the flesh and their punishment set for all Eternity.

And who will be the Judge? Who will be the pre-eminent Figure at these judgments? It will be Jesus Christ, the Righteous. *Acts 17:31* — "He hath appointed a day, in which he will judge the world in righteousness by that man whom he hath ordained; whereof he hath given assurance unto all men, in that he hath raised him from the dead."

Then of course, Christ will be pre-eminent in heaven. When He made man He put him into a good home on earth, but the devil was loose and sin came into that home and ruined it. Now sin covers the whole earth and this world is not a good home any more. But Jesus has gone to prepare a better home. Satan can never enter that home, no sin can cross the threshhold, and sickness and sorrow and death can never touch those who dwell there. And up there Christ will be the pre-eminent figure. All honor and power and glory and majesty shall be His. He will be pre-eminent in heaven.

Now I would like to ask you this question — is Christ pre-eminent in your life? Does He have the first place in your love? Does He reign upon the throne of your heart?

Leonardo da Vinci had just finished painting his great picture, "The Last Supper." He invited another artist in to see the picture. When the artist examined the picture, he said, "What a beautiful cup in the hand of Christ!" Da Vinci quickly seized a brush and painted the cup out of the picture. He said, "I don't want anything in this picture that will detract from the face of Christ." Oh, if there is anything in these little lives of ours which detracts from the glory of Christ, let us cast it out. Let us give Him the pre-eminent place.

Someday soon — it won't be long — you and I will be going out to meet Him. May God help us so to live and so to give Him the pre-eminence that in that day we will hear Him say, "Well done, thou good and faithful servant; enter thou into the joy of thy Lord." And then we shall enter our heavenly home and throughout eternity we shall praise our pre-eminent Lord and Saviour.

Sermon 4

THE CROSS OF CHRIST

Galatians 6:14

Surely you will agree with me when I say that God's biggest man this side of the Lord Jesus Christ was the apostle Paul. He was the finest Christian this world has ever seen. He was the greatest gospel preacher men have ever heard. He was the most marvelous trophy of the grace of God in the history of Christianity. When this great Christian, this great preacher, this great man of God came down toward the end of his earthly days, he looked back over his life and exclaimed, "God forbid that I should glory, save in the cross of the Lord Jesus Christ!" Now I will grant you that he could have gloried in other things. He could have gloried in his ancestry, for he descended from a long line of wonderful people. He could have gloried in his mighty intellect, for he was easily one of the most brilliant men of his day. He could have gloried in the works that he did, for he went up and down the land winning people and building churches for the glory of God. He could have gloried in the things that he wrote, for he left some mighty literature which has blessed people down through the ages. But Paul turned away from all these things, and declared that all of his glory, all of his boast, was in the cross of Christ.

He did not say that he gloried in the virgin birth of Christ, although he, of course, believed in that. He did not glory in the miracles of Christ, although he knew about them. He did not glory in the matchless life that Jesus lived, nor in the great sermons that He preached. Instead, he turned to the central thing for which Jesus came into the world and cried out, "I boast only in the cross of the Lord Jesus Christ!"

And so, as we think of Paul's mighty declaration, we sing today:

> In the cross of Christ I glory
> Towering o'er the wrecks of time.
> All the light of sacred story
> Gathers round its head sublime.

Now why should we glory in the cross today? Why should we preach the cross? Why should we make so much of the cross? It was certainly not a glorious object when Christ died upon it. Death upon the cross meant the most shameful death that a man could die. It meant the greatest humiliation that could be imposed upon a human being. Yet when Jesus died upon that cross, He made it forever glorious. The day He was crucified has become the greatest day in the history of the world. That cross has become the highest symbol that men ever looked upon. The influence of that cross has become the mightiest power in all the world. The little light which was kindled that day upon Calvary has indeed become the Light of the world.

So today in deepest humility, let us kneel at the foot of the cross and find its meaning for our hearts.

I. First, the Cross Expresses the Depth of Human Sin

We think we know something about human sin. We read about it in our newspapers. We see it in the lives of those around us. We find it in our own hearts. But we can never realize the depth of human sin until we go to the cross and realize that our sin crucified the Son of God. Some years ago just before the Christmas season, I saw a crowd of people standing in front of a shoe store. I inquired as to why the crowd had gathered there, and I learned an employee of that store had been discharged that morning. Then he had gone home in anger and secured his pistol. He came back to the store, killed his employer, killed another clerk, wounded another man, and then killed himself. When I think of a tragedy like this, I say to myself, "Now I know something of the awful depth of human sin."

Some years ago I heard an Armenian tell about the atrocities committed against his people by the Turks. These Armenians were stripped naked and crucified upon rows of crosses. Some of them were forced to dig trenches and then they were thrown into these trenches and covered with earth, there to smother. When I heard about these things, I said to myself, "Now, I know some of the awful depths of human sin." You look upon the face of a young woman in a casket. Having fallen into sin and being in deep remorse, she has taken her own life. You are forced to say, "This is what sin will do." You go down to a drunkard's home and you find a broken-hearted wife and little children being deprived of the necessities of life because the husband and father spends all of his earnings upon drink. Then you say, "This is what sin can do."

But, my friends, we know nothing of the awful depth of human sin until you go to the cross. We look upon the One who is dying there and we say, "Who is this that is dying, and why does He die?" And the answer comes back from heaven, "This is My only begotten Son, dying not for His own sin, but for the sins of others." And when you and I come to realize that our sin plucked God's Son out of the Father's bosom and brought Him down to this world to die upon a cruel Roman cross, we come to realize something of the awful depth of our sin.

Let me tell you that sin is no little thing. It is the second biggest thing in the world. The Love of God is the only thing greater. A certain wealthy man in Chicago had a little girl who was desperately ill. He called in many doctors and spent great sums of money for treatments, but the little girl's health did not improve. Finally this man wrote out a check for $20,000 and sent it to the famous Dr. Lorenz of Austria in order to bring the great doctor to Chicago. His treatment was successful and soon the little girl was well and strong again. When you realize the tremendous price this father was willing to pay to see his little girl restored to health, you realize not only how much he loved her, but you realize that there was something fearfully wrong with her. And when we realize the great price that God was willing to pay for our salvation, we realize that there is something wrong with the human race. We come to realize that sin is no little thing. It cost God His very best. So we see that the cross expresses the depth of human sin.

II. The Cross Also Expresses the Highest Love in Heaven and Earth

As we come to the cross, we realize not only the depth of human sin, but the height of divine love. We realize not only how deep a man can go into sin, but how high God can go in His love. "God so loved that He gave. . . ." He gave not the silver and the gold and the diamonds of the earth, although they are His. He gave not the cattle upon a thousand hills, but He gave His only begotten Son for our redemption. In the old horse and buggy days, a young man was engaged to marry a beautiful young woman. One day as he stood on the curb of the street, he saw a runaway horse charging down the road. As he looked closer he saw that his sweetheart was sitting helplessly in the carriage to which the horse was hitched. Without any thought for himself, this man rushed out into the street and grasped the reins. He was finally able to stop the horse and save the one he loved. But in so doing he himself was trampled under foot. The pale, trembling girl got down out of the carriage and rushed around to the place where he lay. As she put her arms under his head and lifted him up, he said to her with his last gasp, "I loved you Mary, didn't I?" In like manner you and I were behind the black runaway horse of sin. We were going down toward death and hell. Then Jesus, without thinking of Himself, rushed out to Calvary and gave His life away for us. Surely, He can say to you and to me, "I loved you, didn't I?"

When a friend tells me that he loves me, I believe it, but when he is willing to suffer in my stead, I know it. We believe that Jesus loves us when we see Him leaving heaven's glory, when we see Him walking His lonely way through this world, when we hear Him praying in Gethsemane. But when He goes to Calvary and dies for us, we know of a truth that He loves us with all of His heart. As we stand at the foot of the cross, we look up into His face and say, "Dear Lord, dost Thou love me?" And He doesn't have to say a word. He just shows us the bleeding wounds that He bears and we know that He loves us more than anyone else ever could love us.

III. THE MESSAGE OF THE CROSS IS THE ONLY MESSAGE OF THE MINISTRY.

Preachers may disagree on many things, but they must never disagree on the fact that the cross should be at the center of their ministry, and in every message which they preach. We are told that there was a time when every rope in the British Navy had a scarlet thread running through the center of it. This thread strengthened and identified the rope. In like manner, our sermons should have as their center the red thread of the precious blood of Jesus Christ. Paul said, "We preach Christ crucified." That is the message which this old world needs today. While we preach on lighter themes, men are going down to death and destruction. The only message of a God-called and divinely-sent minister should be the message of the cross of Christ.

The Cross of Christ

IV. The Cross Is the Place Where Every Need of Mankind Is Met.

Have you had some great sorrow to come into your life? Has some tragedy broken your heart? Then I urge you to come to the cross. Look up into the face of Christ and say to Him, "Oh, thou who hast suffered more than any man has ever suffered, help me in my trouble." And surely He will put His loving arms around you and give you comfort and grace and the peace that passeth all understanding.

Some years ago, just after the loud speakers for radios had been perfected, I was walking down the street of a certain southern city. I heard all the jangled noises and discords of the street. The street cars were rushing by with their cargos of human freight. Men and women were hurrying here and there. And then, above all the jangled noises and discords of the street, I heard a beautiful voice singing a sweet and comforting hymn. Someone had placed a radio loud-speaker just above the door of a radio repair shop and this lovely hymn floated out above all the stress and strain of a busy city street. And if you and I will only listen with the heart, we will be able to hear the sweet voice of Jesus, coming to us above all the discordant notes of life. We can hear Him saying, "I will never leave thee nor forsake thee, I will be with you always. I will give you strength and comfort and grace and cause all things to work together for your good." Yes, Jesus is the answer to every question, the solution to every problem.

Do you have any differences with anybody in the world? Is there someone toward whom you bear malice or ill-feeling? Is there someone to whom you do not speak cordially? Then you ought to bring that difference to the foot of the cross and permit it to be melted in the warmth of His love and sacrifice. A young couple who had a lovely little girl were not able to get along together, and finally their marriage ended in divorce. Then one day the little girl became sick and died. The young father came back for the funeral and out there in the cemetery he and his former wife came together on common ground. It was the common ground of their love for the little girl. When they came together that day, they decided to patch up their differences and try again to make a success of marriage. If you have any difference in your life with anyone, you ought to bring that difference to the area of love which surrounds the cross of Calvary. Surely then these differences can be done away with.

Do you have a life to live? Do you have children to rear? Do you have lost loved ones? Then bring all of these things to the foot of the cross, for it is there where every need of mankind is met.

V. The Way of the Cross Is the Only Way That Men Can Be Saved

Over in London a blind man walked the streets daily, reading a portion of the Bible in Braille print and begging for his living. One day as he was reading the Book of Acts, he lost his place. Nervously he kept running his fingers up and down the page trying to locate the place where he had left off reading. Since he could not find the place, he kept repeating audibly just three words, "None other Name." Some of those who stood by laughed at the blind man's confusion. But there was one young man who did not laugh. This young man had sought salvation and satisfaction in many of the things of the world. But as the blind man repeated these three words, the young man came to realize that there was "none other Name under heaven given among men" whereby he could be saved. He rushed home, fell on his knees by the side of his bed and pouring out his heart to God, he found Christ as his Saviour.

There is no other way of salvation. The way of the cross is the only way.

> I must needs go home by the way of the cross,
> There's no other way but this;
> I shall ne'er get sight of the Gates of Light,
> If the way of the cross I miss.

We are not saved by our good works — we are not saved by our generous gifts. We are not saved by trying to keep the Ten Commandments, nor are we saved by living up to the principles of the Sermon on the Mount. We are not saved by the Golden Rule. We are saved by the substitutionary death of Jesus Christ on the cross, through our repentance for sin and our faith in the Saviour. The religious world is in great confusion today on the matter of salvation. They advocate salvation through form, through creeds, through church membership. But there is no salvation except in this One who died on Calvary's cross.

A ship was sinking out in the middle of the Atlantic Ocean. There were not enough life-belts for all the passengers. A young father put the last life-belt around his wife and little boy and said to his wife: "I will go down to a watery grave, but I want you and our son to be saved. Then when he is old enough to understand, just tell him that his father loved him enough to die in order that he might be saved." The years went by and one day the little boy looked at the picture of his father and then said to his mother, "Mommy, tell me more about Daddy." And the mother told the little boy the story of the shipwreck and of how his father had loved him enough to die in his stead. She finished the story by saying, "Your father died that you might live." My friend, when you come face to face with the picture of your sin, I would tell you again the sweet, wonderful old story of Jesus and His love and I would climax the story by saying, "Jesus died in your stead. He died that you might be saved." The great question therefore of the judgment will be, "What did you do with Jesus who died upon the cross?"

The good man must come to the cross to be saved — the bad man can also come to the cross and find salvation. Some years ago I was holding a meeting in a little mountain town in North Carolina. The pastor of the church walked with me down the street and we stopped at a barber shop. It was a nice shop with ten chairs and ten barbers. I met the young man who owned this shop. When we came out, the pastor told me that this young man was not a Christian. I then decided that I would go to the barber shop each morning and let this young man give me a shave, so that I might have an opportunity to present Christ to him.

So the next morning, while I was in his chair, I invited him to come to the meeting. He showed absolutely no interest in my invitation. The next morning I again pressed the invitation upon him and he said, "My wife said that she would like to go to another revival meeting, so we might come one of these nights." But the young man didn't come that night either. The next morning I said to him, "I am preaching tonight on a subject which I think would be of interest to you. Why don't you come to the service tonight?" He promised that he would come if he could get through work in time.

That night I saw him and his wife enter the church. He sat near the front as I preached my sermon that night. I could see that somehow the Spirit of God was bringing conviction to his heart. However, when the service had ended he rushed out of the church. The next morning I told him that I had seen him in church and hoped that he would return. He said that he would be there again that night. Again he listened to me with rapt attention and again I could see that the note of conviction was written upon his face.

The next morning I said to him, "What are you going to be doing at 2 o'clock this afternoon?" He said, "I will do anything that you ask me to do." He was in trouble. He was under conviction and needed help. So I said to him, "I will be here at 2 o'clock today to take you to ride in your automobile." I came back that afternoon and he was ready to go with me. He gave me the keys to his car and I slipped under the steering wheel. He sat beside me without saying a word. It was a beautiful April day. Springtime had come to the mountains. We drove down the highway a short distance and I stopped the car on the side of the road and talked to this young man about giving his heart to Christ. I read several Scriptures to him, then I leaned my head over the steering wheel and offered a prayer in his behalf. When the prayer was ended I said to him, "Will you do it — will you take Christ as your Saviour?" And he gave me a strong grip of the hand and said to me, "I will take Him as my Saviour right now and I will confess Him before the church tonight."

That night he and his wife both came forward confessing Christ. Before the meeting was over he was visiting other lost men in an effort to win them to the Saviour.

The days went by and he became very active in his church. Then the time came when he felt that God had called him to preach. He sold his barber shop and went away to college to prepare himself for better service for the Lord.

Some years later I was preaching in another state. I told this story and mentioned the man's name and a young couple came up to me at the close of the service saying, "That man is our pastor and he is a wonderful Christian and a fine preacher." When I heard that statement, I went back in my memory to that spring day in the mountains when I told the man about Christ and when he accepted the Lord as his Saviour. He came to the foot of the cross that day — he left his sins there and took the great Saviour as his Saviour. There is no other way of salvation for anyone.

What are you doing about the cross? There is salvation there if you will only look and live. But it isn't enough that God loves you — it isn't enough that Christ died for you — it isn't enough that the Holy Spirit seeks to win you to the side and service of Jesus. You must come to the cross, repenting of your sins and trusting Christ as your personal Saviour. In this way you will be able to appropriate to yourself all that Christ did for you upon the cross.

One of our great preachers tells the following experience. One morning his phone rang and a young man said to him, "Preacher, I want you to be ready to go home with me in three minutes' time." Of course, the preacher must always be ready, so he was in front of the house when the young man drove up. The preacher got into the car and they started down the street at a breakneck rate of speed.

Suddenly the young man cried out, "Oh, preacher, if you know how to pray, please pray now for my little girl. I am afraid that she is dying. Please ask God to let her live."

The preacher said, "I cannot pray in that manner, but I must pray for God's will to be done. Surely I will pray for Him to spare the life of the little one if that can be His will, but if not, I will ask Him to give grace to you and your wife in this time of need."

But the young man said, "I can stand it all right. . . . I am big and strong, but my wife has never been too strong and I am afraid that this blow will kill her."

But the preacher knew that the wife was a Christian, whereas the young husband did not know the Lord. In a few minutes they came to the house and went into the room where the little child lay in her little bed. The young mother was kneeling by the side of the bed, saying a few words first to the little child and then to God. In a few minutes they could see that the end was near. The husband ran out of the room and into the back yard. When the little girl had breathed her last breath, the mother asked the preacher to go out and find her husband. When the preacher approached him in the back yard, the young man said, "It is all over now, isn't it, preacher?" And the preacher replied, "Yes, she has passed away." Then the young man said, "I can stand it all right, but this will kill my little wife." "Let's go in now and see about it," said the preacher.

They went into the house and when they came to the door they stopped for a moment. The little mother was kneeling by the bedside praying and they felt that they were standing on holy ground. She was telling God that it was good to have had the little girl for a few years, if not for many years. She was telling Him that it was better to have loved and lost than never to have loved at all. She was telling the Lord that she would be a better servant because of the life and death of the little one.

In a few minutes she had ended her prayer and the preacher and the husband went into the room. She came over and put her arms around her husband's neck and said to him, "Honey, I am so sorry for you. My heart is broken, but God has sent little bits of sunshine down into my soul. He has given me the comfort and grace which I needed. But I am so sorry for you, because you do not have a Saviour to help you in this time of need." Then the young father turned to the preacher and said, "If God can do that for my wife, I want to take Christ as my Saviour, too." Soon the three of them were kneeling by the bedside and the husband was claiming Christ as his Saviour. His sins were forgiven and the peace that passeth all understanding entered into his heart.

Yes, my friends, Christ meets every need that we have in this life and gives us a hope for the life to come. Why not take Him as your Saviour and follow Him until the day is done and we see Him over yonder in the land of fadeless day?

Sermon 5

THE GREATEST MAN ALIVE TODAY

I Corinthians 15:12-26
(Easter Sermon)

If I were to ask you who is the greatest man alive today, I am sure that I would receive many answers. Someone would point to a mighty statesman like Churchill and say that he is the greatest. Some would point to the president of the United States and say that he is the greatest man alive. Someone would point to Eisenhower, who served his country gloriously for fifty years, and say that he is the greatest man alive. Someone would point to Billy Graham, the matchless evangelist, and say that he is the greatest man alive. But I want to tell you that Jesus Christ is the greatest man alive today. You say, "Oh, but He died on the cross more than nineteen hundred years ago. He is not alive." Ah, but He is! He rose from the dead and lives today at the right hand of God.

Compared with Him all the colossal figures of the ages fade into oblivion. Great empires have risen and fallen. Mighty men have lived and ruled and died. Yet this simple Man, born in a stable, reared in a carpenter's shop, this simple Preacher, this Man who never harmed anyone, this gentle Lover of men, this Man who was killed at Calvary, still lives as the Saviour of men and the inspired Teacher of all ages. How can you explain the continuity of Jesus? How can you explain His strange power over the hearts and minds of men? How can you explain His powerful influence in the world? In just one way — by remembering that He is the Son of God. And though they crucified Him, He burst the bonds of death and the grave and came back to live forever.

Now on this Easter Sunday let us remember that we who believe in Him will go the same route that He took. Of course, if He returns in the air while we are living, we will be taken up to heaven without going through the experience of death. But if He tarries everyone of us is going to die. But that will not be the end. If we believe in Him, we may go down into the grave, but He has made a back door to the grave and we will follow Him up the sunlit hills of glory. Now let's get one thing straight. When a Christian dies, his soul goes up to be with Jesus. We hear Paul saying, "It is better for me to depart and be with Christ." Again we hear him saying, "Absent from the body, present with the Lord." He is teaching us that when a Christian dies, the soul immediately leaves the body and goes up to heaven. The body is then buried to await the resurrection morning. And when Christ comes, we are told that the dead in Christ will rise first. Their bodies will be taken up and changed into the glorious likeness of Christ. Body and soul will be joined and then we shall be forever with the Lord. Only then will our salvation be complete.

I. The Proof of the Resurrection

Jesus died at three o'clock in the afternoon, saying, "It is finished," and "Into thy hands I commend my spirit." Three days go by, lonely and sad days for the disciples. Their Master is dead. There is no use to look forward to happy days in the Kingdom of God, no need to preach any more, no need to do anything but go back to work and forget all about Jesus and His wonderful promises. But they are in for a great surprise. On the third day Jesus got up and walked out of that tomb and is now more alive than ever before. The disciples met Him and touched Him. They talked with Him and ate with Him. They saw Him many times before He told them good-by for a while and ascended into heaven.

1. *We know that He rose from the dead because He had power over death.* While He was here He brought three people back from death unto life. Then He said, "I have power to lay down my life and power to take it up again." And He exercised that power. They could not have killed Him if He had not submitted to them. He could rise from the dead because He had power over death. The grave could not hold Him. He made the earth and every foot of ground. He who made it could not be held captive by it.

2. *We know that He rose from the dead because He was seen of many witnesses.* Peter and James and John and the others had walked with Him for three and a half years. Do you think that they would not recognize Him if He came before them again? They saw Him alive, and because they saw Him they were changed men. Before His death they were cowards. They

The Greatest Man Alive Today

ran away the night before the Crucifixion. One denied that he had ever known Him. But look at them now. They go forth to preach Christ boldly and they give their lives away for Him. Now a dead man couldn't inspire other men to do that. They knew they had a living Saviour.

3. *We know that He rose from the dead because of the prominent place given to the Resurrection in the Bible.* There are two hundred and sixty chapters in the New Testament and the Resurrection is mentioned more than one hundred times. And when the Apostles preached, they centered every message on the fact that Christ had risen and was alive. If I come and preach to you about a Saviour who can do great things and then you learn that death can conquer Him, you would say, "I don't know whether He can help me or not." But when we know that He defeated death and cheated the grave, we say, "That's the One for me. If He could do that, I know that He can save and help me." You rob the Gospel of its power if you deny the Resurrection. The Bible tells us that He rose from the dead, that He ascended on high, that He sits at the right hand of God, making intercession for us, and that He is awaiting the time when He will come back to earth again.

4. *We know that He rose from the dead because of His influence upon the world.* Think of all the hospitals and orphanages and homes for the aged and all the charities and all the institutions organized to help people. All of these came into being because of the influence of Jesus Christ. They don't have these things where His knowledge has never been. We know that a dead man could not inspire other men to do these things. Christ is alive!

We are told that about 98 percent of Americans over eighteen believe in God. But several years ago a group organized the American Association for the Advancement of Atheism. In 1954 they had only three hundred and forty members and these members paid dues of one dollar per year. This means that they contributed $340.00 to the cause of atheism. Many of our church members pay more to the cause of Christ in one year than all of these atheists put together. Christ is alive! And that is the reason that millions of people all over the world love and follow Him. That is the reason that millions of dollars are given to His cause every year.

So let us now rejoice that we have a living Saviour. In the Old Testament days men observed the seventh day of the week in commemoration of a finished creation. Today we celebrate the first day in commemoration of a finished redemption. God did a great thing in creating the world. He did a greater thing in giving us His only begotten Son. To the Bible Christian every Sunday is Easter Sunday. Every week we celebrate the Resurrection. Every day we are to remember that Christ is alive, the greatest Man alive on earth today.

II. THE PROFIT OF THE RESURRECTION

We need a living Saviour. We need Him to do certain things for us, things a dead man can never do. Let us think of some of these things.

1. *We need a living Saviour to save us.* We are sinners, caught in the mire of sin like a man sinking into quicksand. Who can pull us out? Who can save us? There is only One and He is alive. Jesus is His Name. Dr. Samuel Chadwick of England announced a service for infidels only. A large crowd came. They would not sing nor bow their heads in prayer. They heckled the preacher while he brought his message. At the end of the sermon he asked those who wanted to discuss religion to meet him in his study. Nineteen of them came. He said to them, "Suppose that we grant that your philosophy is sufficient for a man of moral character, social position, and economic security. What will you do for those who do not have these things, whose lives have been wrecked by sin?" The spokesman for the group answered, "We would bring them to you, for you have their only hope." Yes, Jesus Christ is the only hope for those who have sinned. This means that He is the only hope for all men, for all have sinned, whether they be rich or poor, great or small, learned or ignorant.

A young research chemist one day accidentally injected into his own veins a drug which he knew had killed in twelve hours every animal it had been used on. No antidote had been found. With a sickening feeling he watched his arm begin to swell. "What shall I do?" he whispered to himself. "This is my last day on earth." He hailed a cab and rushed home to spend his few remaining hours with his family. Suddenly, as the pain mounted, he began to see what the truly valuable things in life were. Not fame and money, but a right relationship to God, and honor and faith and love. It took death to show him the value of the most important things of life. I talk to men about accepting Christ, about getting right with God, about going to church and living for the Lord. And many of them are not impressed. They are thinking too much of this world. Oh, if they only knew that death might be around the corner, they would see things in their true light and do something about it. Yes, we need a living Saviour to save us and we have One who says, "Come unto me." "Him that cometh unto Me, I will in no wise cast out."

2. *We need a living Saviour in time of sorrow.* He is always ready to comfort. Oh, come with your sorrow and look up into His face! Say to Him, "Oh, Thou who didst sweat drops of blood in Gethsemane's garden, Thou who didst suffer on Calvary's cross, remember me, help me." And surely He will reach down and put His loving arms around you and give you the peace which passeth all understanding.

One man said that he had made four trips to the cemetery to put away loved ones. He stated that as he returned home every turn of the wheels seemed to whisper that God's grace was sufficient for his every need. Yes, we have a living Saviour to comfort us in time of sorrow.

3. *We need a living Saviour to answer our prayers.* And we have One, One whose ears are always open to our cries. One who is ready to answer our prayers in the way that is best for us.

A Christian man who was in the real estate business one day took a young couple out to see a house. The house was not much, but the young people were elated. They were in love and they looked forward to fixing up the house and living happily in it. While they were running through the house, the Christian salesman stood in the kitchen and prayed. He prayed that Jesus would always be honored in this house, and that He would take care of this couple and give them happiness. The couple signed the contract and thanked the salesman. He said that from that day on he prayed for every house he tried to sell, that Christ might be honored there. As he brought the Lord into every transaction, it transformed his own life. He was brought to realize that his secular business could be used for the glory of God. One day he said to a preacher, "Why didn't someone tell me long ago how wonderful Jesus is?" Oh, if we pray, if we talk to this living Saviour every day, we will find out how wonderful He is.

4. *We need a living Saviour to guide us in our choices.* Once upon a time an Oriental king dressed up in his fancy uniform and all of his medals every day and strutted up and down before the mirror, admiring himself. He thought only of himself while

his people suffered and starved. One elderly attendant realized that there was some good in the king if he could only be brought to think of something else besides himself. So one night this man removed the mirror and cut a window where the mirror had been. Next morning, when the king came to admire himself, he looked instead through the window and saw his people. He saw a weary mother and her children; he saw tired men bent beneath heavy loads. He saw hungry children exploring garbage cans for food. He even saw a beautiful maiden. Abruptly he removed his uniform, dressed himself in simple clothes, and went out among his people. He learned their needs and set out to relieve their suffering. He even found for himself a beautiful wife.

That's what we need to do. We need to take our eyes off ourselves and look at Jesus and the needs of others. Then we will make the right choices and our lives will be transformed.

5. *We need a living Saviour to take us to heaven.* He said, "I go to prepare a place for you." Heaven is a prepared place for prepared people. We prepare ourselves by faith in Him, then He takes us to heaven at the end of the way.

Do you remember when you were saved? You looked up and cried unto Him to forgive your sins and save you. You were not talking to a dead God. You were talking to a living Saviour and He saved you. Do you remember when you were in sorrow? You asked Him for comfort and He comforted you. You were not talking to a dead man. Do you remember how often you prayed and felt His presence very near? A living Saviour was there. Do you remember when you had an important choice to make? You asked a living Saviour and He guided you aright. Well, the same Saviour who has saved and blessed you all along the way will take you home one of these days.

When General MacArthur left Bataan he said, "I shall return." His soldiers were imprisoned by the Japanese. They waited and waited and thought that he would never come back. But one day some American tanks rolled up to the prison gates and the officer in the front tank commanded that the gates be opened. The Japanese refused to do this, so the officer set his tank at full power ahead and crashed through the gates. Other tanks followed and the Americans took over. Soon the prisoners were shouting all over the camp. But in the back part of the camp there was one man who was too weak to come out. He wondered why all the shouting and noise were going on. Soon a

The Greatest Man Alive Today

buddy came back and told him what had happened. He then picked him up and brought him out into the center of the camp. Then the sick soldier bowed down and thanked God and cried out, "Free! Free! Free at last!"

Death may conquer us, the grave may hold our bodies for a while. But one day Jesus will come and our bodies will be raised in glory. Then we will go up to be with Him forever, free forever. So on Easter Sunday let us thank God for a living Saviour who saves us and takes us to heaven. And let us here highly resolve that we are going to be more faithful to Him than ever before.

Sermon 6

THE GOSPEL OF CHRIST

Romans 1:16

The apostle Paul was the choicest gospel preacher this world ever knew. He counted it a great privilege to tell everywhere the story of Christ and what the Lord had done for him. He told the story in Jerusalem, where the Jews were so bitterly opposed to him. He told the story in Asia Minor, where they beat him and left him for dead. He told the story in Athens, the cultural center of the ancient world. He told the story in Rome, the city which trusted in its military strength and forgot God.

Before he went to Rome, Paul wrote a letter to the Christians there. He longed to preach the Gospel in this powerful center. He knew that all the power of Rome would be against him, but he said, "I am not ashamed to go. I will put the Gospel of Christ up against all the sin and superstition of Rome."

Now as Paul looked back over his life, he must have thought about many things of which he was ashamed. He thought about how he persecuted Christians and put them to death. He thought about Stephen and how he stood by and watched them stone this good man to death. He thought about how he had made havoc of the church. He remembered how he had hurt Christ in hurting His followers. But now he is a changed man. Christ is his whole life. He loved Christ more than he loved himself. He was trying his best to make up for what he had done before he was converted. He had tried the Gospel upon himself and it had worked. He had seen it work in the lives of many others. No wonder he said, "I am not ashamed of the Gospel of Christ."

I. Like Paul, We Should Be Ashamed of Many Things

1. *We should be ashamed of our sins.* We have been sinning ever since we were born, and some of our sins have been as black as night. Oh, as we look back over the pathway of life, we wish that it were a clear pathway, but we see that it has been filled with many sins. Many times we have gotten off the track.

Often the devil has tripped us up. Oh, what we might have been if we had not sinned so often! And who is to blame for our sins? Not our parents, not our preachers, not our teachers. We alone are to blame. Today we ought to be ashamed of every spot of sin in our lives.

2. *We should be ashamed of our mistakes.* We have often done and said the wrong thing. We have gone according to our own wisdom instead of seeking the guidance of God. We have not prayed enough. We have thought that we could work things out alone. Oh, how many errors we have made! We are far from perfect in God's book. Haven't you often said, "Oh, if I just hadn't done this or said that! Oh, if I had only been a little more patient and a little more Christ-like on that occasion." Yes, we often make mistakes. The biggest mistake I ever made was when I ran ahead of God. All of us should be ashamed of our mistakes.

3. *We should be ashamed of our failures.* We have often failed miserably, simply because we did not depend upon God. Let a man with even one talent go in the strength of the Lord and he will win. But we often fail because we leave God out of our plans and actions.

4. *We should be ashamed of the small progress we have made in our Christian lives.* From the day that we are born again we ought to be growing in grace until the day that we die. But some of us are no better Christians than the day that we were saved. We have grown physically, mentally, socially, and financially, but we have not grown spiritually. Sometime ago a group of preachers on a train were discussing their own shortcomings. The oldest preacher among them said, "The biggest fault with us is that we do not pray enough." That is true of everyone of us. We know the power of prayer, but we do not use it.

We are not consecrated enough, we don't live close enough to the Lord, we pray too little and neglect our Bible too much. Jesus is not always first with us. We let the world creep in and take over. We ought to be ashamed that we have not grown in grace as we should.

5. *We should be ashamed of the little service we have given to Christ.* When He has needed us, we have been too busy to serve Him. When we need Him, He is always ready to help. You may be a child of God, you may be a member of a good church, but what are you doing for God?

When you go to Niagara Falls, you watch millions of gallons

of water pour over the falls every minute. You begin to think of all the wasted power that is there. But not all of this power is wasted. Much of it is harnessed and used for the benefit of mankind. But our powers are wasted, powers which ought to be used for God. Scores of our church members ought to come forward and say, "I know that you need my help in the church, what can I do?"

When we were building our new educational building I made an appeal for more workers to serve in the Sunday School. After the service one man said to me, "I can't teach a class or do anything like that, but I can give the money to equip that building." Consequently he gave thousands of dollars for this worthy cause. When we were building our new church auditorium another man said, "I am not a church leader, but I am planning to give my home to the church and move into an apartment." He gave the church his home and it was sold for thousands of dollars and this money put into the building fund. You may not be able to do this, but you can give what you are able to give. This is one way to serve God.

6. *We should be ashamed that we have not always carried out our good intentions.* On New Year's Day we make our solemn resolutions. We say, "I am going to live closer to God. I am going to be more faithful to my church." Or maybe in some high hour you have said, "I am going to be a better Christian." But you have forgotten these vows. This ought to cause shame. They tell us that "the road to hell is paved with good intentions." We ought to be ashamed of all of these things and many others which have kept us from being what we should be.

II. BUT WE CAN SAY WITH PAUL, "I AM NOT ASHAMED OF THE GOSPEL OF CHRIST"

1. *We are not ashamed of it's Author, Jesus Christ.* The human race did not and could not produce Jesus. If this were possible, why doesn't the human race produce another One like Him? Only God could produce such a person. Christ was truly His "only begotten Son."

A recent bishop said this, "Biblical evidence seems to favor the assumption that Joseph was the human father of Jesus." But the bishop doesn't give any Scripture to support such a position. The Bible plainly states that Jesus was *not* the Son of Joseph. He was God's Son, brought into the world by the virgin Mary. We have no reason to be ashamed of Him.

The Gospel of Christ 57

General Robert E. Lee's men were devoted to him. One night around the campfire some of his soldiers were discussing evolution. One of them said, "We soldiers might be descended from monkeys, but only God could make Marse Robert." We are products of humanity, but only God could make Jesus Christ. He is the Son of God, the King of kings, and the Lord of lords, the Rose of Sharon, and the Lily of the Valley. He is the fairest among ten thousand and the One altogether lovely.

> No mortal can with Him compare
> Among the sons of men,
> Fairer is He than all the fair
> Who fill the heavenly train.

A farmer and his wife sent their son to a university, where he fell in with a group of snobbish students. One day the father felt that he could go no longer without seeing his son. So he said, "Mother, I want to see our boy. I am going to ride over to the university and see him." She packed his lunch, he hitched the horse to the buggy, and started out on the long trip. He arrived at the campus in late afternoon. Suddenly he saw his son coming down the street with two other students. The old farmer, dressed in overalls, got out of the buggy and hurried to meet his son. As he started to throw his arms around the boy, the foolish, ungrateful son said, "I don't know you, sir." Then the boy turned his back upon his father and went away with the other students. The broken-hearted father made his way home in sorrow. This boy was ashamed of his father, but there is no reason on earth for us to be ashamed of Jesus.

Jesus is the Light of the world, He is the Great Shepherd of the sheep. He is the answer to every question, the solution to every problem, the explanation of every mystery. He is the One who was and is and is to be. He is the high and holy One. He inhabits eternity. He is the Lamb slain from the foundation of the world. He is the One who died on the cross for all men. He is the One who rose again, ascended into heaven and who now sits at the right hand of God. He is the One who is coming again to judge all men and to reign forever and ever. No, we should not be ashamed of Him.

Why should we be ashamed of Him? Look at His character. There was no sin in anything that He did or said or thought. There are plenty of flaws in us, but none in Him. He looked down from His throne above and saw us as lost and on the way to hell. He laid aside the robe of royalty and came down and loved us and poured out His blood for us. Then He opened His arms and said, "Him that cometh to Me, I will in no wise cast out." And we came to Him and He forgave us and transformed us and set our feet upon a rock. He put a song in our hearts and hope in our souls. No, we can never be ashamed of Jesus.

2. *We are not ashamed of the message in the Gospel.* It is the only message that has any saving power. Babylon said, "Eat, drink and be merry." Rome said, "Pleasure and power will make you happy." Germany said, "Might is right." Wall Street says, "Pile up your money." The modernist says, "Every man has within himself a spark of divinity." The formalist says, "There is power in these rituals." But all these messages fail. There is no power of God in them. A man dies forever who rejects this message. The church dies which fails to preach it.

Sometime ago a lady said to me, "I am going over to hear Dr. So-and-so. They tell me that his sermons are just shot through with philosophy." But philosophy does not save. This preacher lived in a city of fifty thousand people for eight years and in all of that time he had only two converts. I heard another preacher give his testimony at a pastor's conference. He said, "My church auditorium seats 1,200 people. Sometime ago we were having one hundred people in the morning and about thirty at night. I cried out to God about the situation and He opened my eyes to the fact that I was not preaching the Gospel. Humbled and beaten, I went back to the pulpit and preached Christ. I said to the people, 'You are going to hell if you do not accept Christ as your Saviour.' Before long I was preaching to large congregations both morning and night. We had eighteen additions to our church last Sunday." We need never be ashamed of the Gospel for there is power in it.

3. *We are not ashamed of the fruits of the Gospel.* Jesus said, "By their fruits ye shall know them." The Gospel has certainly borne fruit. When Christ died there was only a handful of believers in the world. Now there are millions.

The modernist tells us how to improve the world, but he doesn't tell us that first you must improve the men who are in the world. This is done only when men heed the message of the Gospel and repent and turn to Christ. If you have something that will lift the yoke of sin from the necks of men, you have something good. The Gospel does this. It bears fruit.

In 1893 the World Congress of Religions met at the Chicago

Fair. The representative of each religion told the merits of his particular faith. The Mohammedan, the Confucionist, the Buddhist, and others spoke of their religion. Then the Christian said, "Is there anything in your religion that will help a man get rid of sin?" All the other speakers were strangely silent. Then the Christian triumphantly said, "Christianity has the answer. 'The blood of Jesus Christ his Son cleanses us from all sin.' " He won the day.

Some years ago I conducted a revival meeting in a church in a Southern city. A certain man came every night and eventually trusted Christ as his personal Saviour. I was leaving the city at a very early hour when the meeting had been finished, but even at this early hour the man came down to the train to bid me good-by. He said this to me, "For 25 years I have been a drinking man. I heard the Gospel this week and was saved. This is the first clear week I have had in 25 years. I am going to be a better man, I am going to live for the Lord." Christ and the Gospel had borne fruit. In another city where I was pastor a man came to church and was gloriously saved. He gave this testimony, "One Sunday night I was so despondent that I was on the way to commit suicide. But it was summer time and the windows of your church were open. I stopped outside one of these windows and heard the Gospel of hope. I gave my heart to Christ and now I take Him and His word with me everywhere." Oh, the Gospel has power to change lives.

The greatest lives of the world have been produced by the Gospel. Paul was the chief of sinners, but the Gospel made him the chief of saints. Peter was the cursing fisherman, but the Gospel made him a mighty preacher. Bunyan was a swearing tinker, but the Gospel made him a great author. Luther was a frigid formalist, but the Gospel made him a mighty reformer. It takes more than a dainty, sugar-sweet, little message to produce a Judson, a Livingston, a Moody, a Spurgeon. Yes, there is power in the Gospel.

4. *Finally, we are not ashamed of the goal of the Gospel.* Heaven is that goal. Heaven is the end of all God's processes. It is Christ's purpose to save and bless here and at the end to take us to a city that is bright and fair and sweet. I am not ashamed to say that I expect to go to heaven, because I have heeded the message of the Gospel. A woman told me this story about her little granddaughter. The child was crippled and was not able to hold her own with the other children. She took the

little girl to a party one day and the little one clung to her hand while the other children played. When the refreshments were announced, the other children ran for the ice cream. This little girl started toward the table, but the other children jostled her and pushed her around. She finally got her ice cream, but was afraid that she would drop it. The grandmother saw the agony on the child's face and went over to her. The child put the ice cream aside and stumbled into her grandmother's arms and safety. We are jostled about by life, but some day we will lay everything else aside. We will see Jesus and melt in His arms, where we will find peace and rest. That's the goal of the Gospel.

You and I can both preach this glorious Gospel. You don't have to mount a pulpit to do it. You can support the Gospel with your prayers and money here and around the world. You can witness to those who know Him not. The greatest sermon ever preached is a consecrated life.

One day Sternberg the artist was requested by a priest to paint a picture of the crucifixion. He agreed to do so, but since he knew nothing of Christ, he had to read his New Testament. He painted the picture, but felt that it wasn't too good, so he left it in his studio. One day a gypsy girl came to the studio to sit as a model. She stopped in front of the picture of Christ and the crucifixion and said, "Who is that man?" The artist then told her the story of the death of Christ. Then she asked him, "Did He do all of this for you?" Sternberg managed to stammer out the word "Yes." "Then," she said, "You must love Him very much for doing all of this for you." He could not get this thought out of his mind. Each day she said the same thing. One night he could not sleep. He got out of bed, read the story again, then fell upon his knees and accepted Christ. He tore up the old picture and painted a better one.

Years later he received a message saying that a dying gypsy woman wanted to see him. When he called upon her he found her to be the same gypsy who had served as his model when she was a little girl. The dying woman looked up and said, "Do you still love the One who died for you?" And the artist answered from his heart, "Yes, I love Him, and He died for you, too." Before she passed away she had given her heart to the Saviour. But that is not the end of the story. This picture was hung in a national gallery. One day the artist saw a man gazing at it intently and weeping. He went forward and led this man to

Christ. The man was Count Zinzendorf, who later founded the Moravian Church.

Oh, Jesus died for you, too! Do you love Him? If you do, you will paint His image with your life, then others will come to love Him also.

Sermon 7

HAVE YOU SEEN JESUS LATELY?

John 12:21

When a man does the unusual, the people flock to see him. When John the Baptist came preaching, he was so unusual in manner and message that the cities emptied themselves and came out to hear him. When Lindberg got into a small plane and flew across the Atlantic Ocean in thirty-three and a half hours, tremendous crowds greeted him wherever he went. When Admiral Byrd came back from the South Pole, the people thronged Broadway to see him. When the Kennedys were in Paris and Vienna and London, thousands of people lined the streets to catch a glimpse of them.

Now if this is true of these people, it is more so of Jesus Christ. He had done unheard-of things. He had made the blind to see, the lame to walk, the deaf to hear. He had cleansed the lepers and even raised the dead back to life again. As His fame spread, the crowds flocked to see and hear Him. Thousands of them followed in His wake. Now at the feast in Jerusalem, some Greeks wanted to get up closer to Him. They had heard of His mighty works and they wanted to get better acquainted with Him. So they came to the disciples and said, "We want to see Jesus." They saw Him and they talked with Him and I am sure they were blessed by being in His presence. I hope that they put their trust in Him for time and eternity.

You and I have never seen Him with the eye of flesh, but we have seen Him by faith. We have seen Him walking the Judean hills. We have seen Him sitting upon the mountain delivering the greatest sermon ever heard. We have seen Him praying in Gethsemane. We have seen Him with bloody back in Pilate's court. We have seen Him hanging upon Calvary's Cross. We have seen Him leaving the tomb and later ascending into Glory. But have you seen Him lately? Let's see if we can't catch a fresh glimpse of Him today. Don't look at the minister, look past him to the Master. Don't look at the servant, look past him to the

Saviour. Come and say with the Greeks of old, "We would see Jesus." Come and say with the disciples, "Show us the Father and it will suffice us."

I. Why Should We Want to See Jesus?

1. *We want to see Him because of His greatness.* When the captains and the kings of this world come our way, we rush to see them. But the greatest men of the world are mere pygmies beside the Lord Jesus Christ. "No mortal can with Him compare among the sons of men."

Everything about Him was great. He was great in His pre-existence, for He lived before He was born. He was great in prophecy, for all the prophets pointed to His coming. He was great in His birth, for He was born as no other. He lived in heaven without a human mother, and He was born into the world without a human father. He was great in His life, for "He went about doing good." He was great in His death, for He gave His life for those who had no life. He was great in His resurrection, coming to life from the dead, as no one else could ever do. He was great in His ascension when He went back home to heaven. He is great in the work that He is now doing for us in heaven. He is great in the promise of His return and His eternal Glory.

Yes, He was the greatest character the world has ever known. He is the brightest light that ever shone. He is the mightiest power the world ever felt. Yes, we want to see Him simply because of His greatness.

2. *We want to see Him because He is the Son of God.* He was not a rich man's son, nor an earthly king's son, but He was God's Son, His Only Son. A certain man had been away from home a long time. His little girl looked longingly at her father's picture and said, "Mother, I wish that Daddy would come down out of that frame." That is what Jesus did. He came down out of heaven and became real to men.

He said, "He that hath seen Me hath seen the Father." For centuries men had cried out for a sight of God. They wanted to know the kind of being that He was. And when Jesus came, God was revealed in His Son.

3. *We want to see Him because of what He did for us.* The blind man who has been cured by a doctor and given his sight wants to see that doctor first of all. The prisoner who has been set free by the governor wants to see his liberator first of all.

Oh, Jesus set us free! He gave us our spiritual eyesight. He has done and will do a thousand other things for us. Surely we want to see Him for this reason. He said, "I must go to Jerusalem and die." And all the time He was thinking of us. When He sweat blood in Gethsemane He was thinking of us. When He received the scourge in Pilate's court He was thinking of us. When the crown of thorns was pressed down upon His brow, He was thinking of us. And on the cross when He cried, "It is finished," He was thinking of us. And because He thought of us and died for us, we want to see Him.

4. *We want to see Him because He is our Mediator.*

Here we are living in a hard old world. We are battered and bruised on every side. Isn't it a comfort to know that up in heaven there is One who is praying for us? We read that "He ever liveth to make intercession for us."

The Bible tells us that "there is one mediator between God and man, the man, Christ Jesus." It is not "*a* man" but "*the* Man." We don't approach God through a priest, through a church, or through a human being, but through Jesus Christ. The veil is rent in twain and we go to the heart of God through the Lord Jesus Christ. Oh, there are so many reasons why we want to see Jesus today!

II. How Can We See Jesus Today?

1. *We can see Him by looking into the Bible.* The Old Testament points its finger at Him. The first prophecy in the Bible tells of how He will bruise the head of Satan. Isaiah draws a perfect picture of Him when he says, "He was wounded for our transgressions, he was bruised for our iniquities; the chastisement of our peace was upon him, and with his stripes we are healed."

Every page in the New Testament tells us about Jesus. John the Baptist says, "Behold the Lamb of God that taketh away the sin of the world." And that is just what we are doing all the way through the New Testament. We are beholding Jesus, the Lamb of God. The Bible pictures Jesus Christ. It is a book so simple that any who seek the right way may understand. It is so difficult that the greatest scholars can't pick it to pieces.

2. *We can see Him in prayer.* We get closer to heaven on our knees than at any other time. 'Tis then that earthly things fade away and we look into the face of the Lord. Close your eyes, forget all else, look up with your soul. Then you will catch a glimpse of Him whose glory fills all of heaven.

3. *We can see Jesus in nature.* In the spring every bursting bud reminds us of the One who burst the bonds of the tomb and came forth to live forever. In the summer, as we look upon the flowers, we are reminded of Him who is the Rose of Sharon and the Lily of the Valley. In the fall, when the leaves are turning, we are reminded of One who never changes. He is "the same yesterday, and today, and for ever." At night when the stars fill the sky, we are reminded of the bright and morning Star. At sunrise we are reminded of the Sun of Righteousness, rising with healing in His wings. At sunset we are reminded of Him who never sleeps and who never leaves us.

4. *We can see Jesus in the lives of Christians.* Sometime ago I heard a man say of an aged preacher, "You can see the good Lord shining in his face." I have looked upon a beautiful Texas sunset and for an hour after that time a resplendent afterglow filled the sky. Jesus has gone from this earth, but we can still see Him in the shining eyes and faces of those who love Him.

We must be careful right here. Can anyone see Jesus in you? The world is looking for Him. They will not look for Him in the Bible nor in nature, but they will look for Him in you and me. How tragic when they can't see Him there. Can people see Jesus in your speech, in your actions, in your attitudes?

> Let others see Jesus in you,
> Let others see Jesus in you,
> Keep telling the story, be faithful, be true,
> Let others see Jesus in you.

5. *We can see Jesus in divine services.* People need Jesus so much today. They don't find Him in the world, so they come to church to catch a glimpse of Him. I have often gone to church and come away dry and disappointed, because Jesus was not exalted. I have gone to church at other times and have come away with my spirit singing, because I had seen Jesus in sermon and in song. May God blow this house of worship down when men come here and fail to see Jesus. May God still the preacher's voice when people can no longer see Jesus in his sermons.

III. WHAT KIND OF A VISION SHOULD WE GET OF JESUS?

1. *We ought to see Him as our Saviour.* The world is filled with thousands of people who have never had an experience of saving grace. They have never met Christ and had their sins washed away. They have never entered the family of God. They have never become children of the heavenly King. Thrice-blessed

are you if you have had that experience, if you have been born again. If not, "Seek ye the Lord while He may be found," for some day it will be too late.

The man without Christ walks alone. He fights the battle of life alone and is on the way to eternal death. But Jesus invites you to walk with Him. He will help you over all the rough places of life, and bring you at the end of the way to the sunlit hills of glory.

2. *We ought to see Him as our Lord and Master.* It is wonderful that He has saved us, but are you content with that? You are not properly related to Him until He is your Lord and Master, until he is the absolute sovereign of your life. Dr. Carl Bates tells of an old man who said, "When I die, put these words on my tombstone, 'Here lies a man for whom Christ died and who during his lifetime tried to make it up to Him.'" That's the way we ought to feel. We ought to be so grateful to Him that we will not simply be contented to be saved and have our names on the church roll book. We ought to let Him take precedence over everything else and everybody else in life.

3. *We ought to see Him as our Comforter.* Isaiah 66:13 — "As one whom his mother comforteth, so will I comfort you." Here is a tender picture. The mother takes a brokenhearted, weeping child in her arms and comforts him as only a mother can. And in like manner, Jesus is a Comfort for every brokenhearted child of His.

Many years ago I heard Harry Lauder sing in North Carolina. He had a heart so jolly that he set the world to laughing. One night as he was about to go on the stage in a London theater, he received a message telling him that his son had been killed in battle in France. He cancelled the engagements which would have paid him great sums and went to France to sing for the soldiers. In a later magazine article he told the secret which Christ gives to those who love Him. He said, "When sorrow comes, there are three things that you can do. You can grow sour on the world, you can drown your sorrow in drink, or you can take it to God. My wife and I took our sorrow to God and there we found our comfort."

4. *We ought to see Him as our daily Helper.* He said that He would be with us alway, even unto the end of the way. So wherever men live, wherever human hearts beat, wherever souls struggle in the darkness, there you will find Jesus. You have only

to reach out to Him to feel the touch of His hand and know that He is there.

A preacher went one day to see a banker who was a member of his church. A white card was hung upon the banker's door and the secretary asked the preacher to wait. He had to wait a half hour. Then the card came down and the preacher was invited into the banker's office. The banker said, "I apologize to you for keeping you waiting. When that white card is on the door, my secretary knows that I am not to be disturbed. I had a difficult problem facing me, and I had to talk to God. I have found that there is not a trial in a banker's life that God cannot meet." Yes, whatever your business, He promises to be with you always.

5. *We ought to see Him as our coming King.* He said that He would come again. We don't know the day nor the hour, but when He comes I want Him to find me faithful and busy for Him. Oh, if we only believed that His coming was near, we would loosen our hold upon the world, turn our backs upon some of the things that we are doing, and take a tighter grip upon God and a greater interest in His work.

6. *Finally, we ought to see him as our final Judge.* When He comes, He will bring Christians before the Judgment Seat and judge their works. What is going to happen to your works? Will they stand the fires of judgment, or will they be burned to a crisp and you be saved just "as if by fire"?

> Only one life, 'twill soon be past;
> Only that which is done for Jesus will last.

You church members who are giving your lives away to every worldly organization and institution are going to lose your reward in that day. Oh, I plead with you to give your lives to the things that count for God!

What about you, lost friend? You will probably live a little longer. You will work at your job, build your home and rear your family. But some day you are going to die and face the judgment. What then, oh soul, what then?

At the close of World War I, a chaplain was talking to a group of soldiers. He asked one of them this question: "What was the best lesson that you learned over there?" And the man replied, "I learned that one man loved me more than he loved his own life." "Tell me about it," said the chaplain. And then the soldier told him how that he and his buddy had been standing in a trench when a deadly hand grenade was thrown in.

They knew that both of them would be instantly killed. But his buddy flung his own body over the hand grenade and was blown to bits, thus saving his friend's life. The soldier then said to the chaplain, "I am alive today because he loved me and died for me. I am going to seek to live in the future so as to be worthy of that love."

But there was One who loved us more than that. His Name was Jesus. While we were yet sinners, He died to save us. God grant that we shall seek to live so that in some small manner we will be worthy of that love.

Sermon 8

THE HOPE OF THE WORLD

Luke 4:14-22a

I like to hear great gospel preachers as they proclaim the unsearchable riches of Christ. It has been my privilege to hear many of the more prominent preachers of our day. But as I look back over the years I think of others whom I wish I could have heard. I think of Spurgeon, the matchless preacher of England, who held great congregations in his hand as he talked about the Lord Jesus. I think of Dwight L. Moody, the uneducated American evangelist who broke the king's English, but who also broke countless thousands of hearts for Christ. I think of Talmadge, the eloquent orator, whose eloquence always centered in the Saviour.

But oh, how wonderful it would have been to hear Jesus. On a certain Sabbath day He enters the synagogue and mounts the pulpit. Every eye is upon Him. The people who are there nudge each other and say, "Isn't this Joseph's son? What will He do? What will He say?" Jesus takes one look at the faces of those in His congregation. He sees all the sorrow and despair written there. He thinks of His mission upon the earth and we hear Him saying, "The Spirit of the Lord is upon me, because he hath appointed me to preach the gospel to the poor; he hath sent me to heal the brokenhearted, to preach deliverance to the captives, and recovering of sight to the blind, to set at liberty them that are bruised, to preach the acceptable year of the Lord."

Here is an old tired, sinful world. But standing in that pulpit that day is the Hope of the world. Sometime ago twelve hundred men gathered together in a certain place. The preacher who was to speak to them said, "I want you to be very frank with me. I want you to give me every objection to Christianity that you have in your minds." One man said, "Church members live inconsistent lives, they do not live up to their profession." This is certainly true. Another man said that preachers were not all that they ought to be. This also is true. Another man called attention to the hypocrites in the church. Finally twenty-seven objections to Christianity were made by these men. Then the preacher said, "Fellows, all that you have said is true, but I notice one thing. You did not say one word against Jesus Christ."

There is nothing wrong with Him. Every one of us must say with Pilate, "I find no fault in this just man." Everything about Him is beyond reproach. He was wonderful in His birth, wonderful in His life, wonderful in His miracles, wonderful in His sermons, wonderful in His death, resurrection, and ascension. He is wonderful in His coming again. Suppose Jesus had never come. Suppose that the angels had never sung on the Judean hills. Suppose that there had been no star over Bethlehem. Suppose that there had been no sermon on the mount, no transfiguration, no Calvary. Suppose there had been no resurrection morning, and no ascension day. Oh, where would this world be? It would be sunk in darkness and in helplessness.

It was a great event when Adam was created. That was a great day when Moses led the children of Israel out of the land of Egypt. That was a wonderful day when David wrote the twenty-third Psalm. It was a great occasion when Columbus discovered America. But the greatest event ever witnessed by man or directed by God was the coming of Jesus Christ into this world. Now let's see what His coming meant to humanity in the way of hope.

I. Jesus Came and Gave a New Appraisal of Human Life.

When He came into the world He found the unhappiest conditions that any man had ever faced. The majority of people were slaves. There was a few rich people and many poor, and the poor were trodden under foot by the rich. Children meant very little to anyone. Herod killed all those under two years of age in Bethlehem in one day. Women had a very lowly place — they were little more than slaves. Did these conditions touch Jesus? Yes! In His first public sermon He said, "I have come to help you. My heart is breaking for you. I have a message of hope for you."

A few months pass by and John the Baptist is languishing in prison. Doubts begin to fill his mind, so he sends a messenger to Jesus to say, "Art thou He that should come, or do we look for another? Art thou the Christ, the Messiah?" And Jesus sent back this answer, "Go and tell John that the blind can see, the lame are made to walk, the lepers are cleansed, the deaf hear, the dead are raised and the poor have the Gospel preached unto them." This answer showed that mankind was very close to His heart.

The poor people were devoted to Him. We read that the "common people heard Him gladly." They followed Him as their best friend. He saw their needs and said unto them, "Be not anxious. God knows all about you and He cares for you." The rich people loved Him, too, for He was no respecter of persons. Nicodemus became His friend and spoke out in the Sanhedrin in His behalf. Joseph lent Him his tomb to lie in when they took Him down from the cross. John had influence at his trial and Matthew made a feast in His honor. I am trying to say that Jesus is interested in everyone, whether they be rich or poor, good or bad, educated or ignorant. Everyone means something to Jesus.

There are few slaves now in the world. Children are loved and cared for. Women have a high place. We have hospitals and orphanages and homes for the aged, all because Christ set a high value upon people. James Martineau has well said, "Jesus Christ must be called the regenerator of the human race. The world has changed and Jesus is the One who changed it."

But remember this – though He was interested in the body, He was much more interested in the soul. He was interested in the earthly lives of people, but more so in their heavenly lives. He was concerned about the ills of the flesh, but more so about the sins of the soul. The same thing is true of Him today. He knows that the body lasts only a few years, but that the soul lives on forever. He wants to see our souls saved. When He came into the world He was interested in every aspect of human life and He gave a new appraisal and value to life.

II. JESUS CAME AND GAVE A MESSAGE OF HOPE CONCERNING OUR LOVED ONES WHO HAVE DIED.

Before He came, there was no light beyond the grave. All was darkness and mystery. For endless centuries men had marched in an unbroken column toward the shadows. And of all the millions who had gone down into the grave, not one had come back. In all the world there was not one empty grave. There was no voice from the beyond. But Jesus came and said, "There is a back door for the grave and it opens into heaven for all who believe. Fear not, you will see your loved ones again, for I am the resurrection and the life. Whosoever believeth in Me, though he were dead, yet shall he live."

Victor Hugo said, "The nearer I reach the end, the plainer do I hear the immortal symphonies of the worlds which invite me. It is marvelous, but it is simple."

Listen to some Scriptures on this subject: "Blessed are the dead which die in the Lord, for they rest from their labours and their works do follow them." And again, "Absent from the body, present with the Lord." And another, "Thus shall we ever be with the Lord." And again, "I go to prepare a place for you, and if I go and prepare a place for you, I will come again and receive you unto myself, that where I am, there you may be also." And then we have Paul's immortal words, "For me to live is Christ, and to die is gain."

Therefore, when we say farewell to our loved ones, we can say with the song,

> Asleep in Jesus, blessed sleep
> From which none ever wakes to weep.
> A calm and undisturbed repose,
> Unbroken by the last of foes.

Two United States senators talked often about the future life. They found no reason to believe that there was a life beyond the grave. They left the Senate at the same time and did not meet again until twenty-five years later. When they did meet one senator said to the other, "Do you have any light?" And the other senator replied, "No, do you?" And the first senator sadly said, "No, I have no light." But there is a light. Jesus said, "As I live, so shall ye live, if ye believe in Me." As we hear those words we look beyond the river of death and know that our loved ones are safe in the arms of Jesus.

Are you afraid of death and the future life? Are you concerned about your loved ones whom you have loved long since and lost a while? Then let Jesus comfort you. He has taken them down into the valley, but He has also led them up the hill that leads to God and heaven.

III. JESUS GAVE AN ANSWER TO THE UNIVERSAL QUESTIONS OF MANKIND.

1. *First, what kind of a God do we have?* Does He love us? Does He care for us? How does He feel about us? There are more than two billion people in the world. Is He interested in one little finite human being? And Jesus, sweet, loving, tender

The Hope of the World

and forgiving, says, "He that hath seen Me hath seen the Father. As you see Me loving, lifting and blessing, you know the kind of a Father that God is. He cares for the lilies of the field. He notes the sparrow's fall — and you are worth more than many sparrows. Yes, God cares for you."

Yonder is a king sitting in his council chamber with his cabinet gathered around him. They are discussing the great matters of state. Then his little girl comes running into the room. She trips and falls nearby and begins to weep. Doesn't the king rush over to pick her up and to wipe away her tears? Yes, he does and it elevates him in our estimation. God is yonder on His throne. He is busy running the universe, but when we fall and cry out, He rushes to help us. That's the kind of a God He is.

A missionary tells about going into a heathen temple in India. A little woman came into the temple with a sick and emaciated child in her arms. She lifted the little child up and began to pray. Then the missionary said to her, "To whom are you praying?" And she answered, "I don't know. But there ought to be someone out there somewhere who would hear a mother's cry and save her child and keep her heart from breaking." Oh, little mother with a broken heart, there is One who cares! And His name is Jesus. Oh, soul bowed down in grief, He knows about your sorrow! Oh, friend burdened with sin, He wants to wash that sin away! Yes, Jesus came to tell us that God is a loving Father.

2. *Another question — how can one who is marred with sin get into right relationship with God?* A poor, broken man comes to Jesus and says, "I am a sinner, I am out of harmony with God. Can you help me?" And Jesus answers, "Yes, come unto Me and I will save you. No man cometh unto the Father but by Me. I am the way, and the truth and the life." And at last, mankind has found its way to God. We come to Him only through faith in Jesus Christ the Saviour.

When the great temple of Karnak came tumbling down, they found that a flaw in just one stone had caused the downfall. So your life may be very beautiful and wonderful and you may be very talented, but the flaw of sin is there. You need to come to Jesus, for He will erase every sin and transform your life.

Years ago on Lincoln's birthday a cartoon appeared in many of our papers. This cartoon pictured a log cabin at the bottom and the White House at the top. A ladder extended from the log cabin to the White House, and the caption of the picture was, "The ladder is still there." Earth is down here and Heaven and God are up there. Jesus is the ladder. And anyone who will climb that ladder will find his way to God and heaven.

A poor man from Europe came to the United States. He began to save his money, hoping to bring his wife and boy over here to be with him. Then he received the sad news that his wife had died and the little boy was left alone. He took all of his money and sent for the little boy. The kindly neighbors tied a ticket around the boy's neck, and also a card giving the father's name and address in the United States. They put him on a ship bound for America. Everyone on the ship was very kind to the little boy and when he reached New York, a good woman met him and put him on the train. She then wired the father telling him at what hour the boy would arrive. That night the train pulled into a little station and the little boy leaped into the arms of his father. That is a picture of God. We are out in sin, but He is longing for us to come to Him. "As many as received Him, to them gave He the power to become the sons of God."

3. *Another question — how may I make my life count, and how may I find happiness?* Jesus tells us plainly that our happiness will not come from the things which we possess. He said that if we would find life, we must lose it for His sake.

Napoleon said, "I will get power. I will climb to the heights and then I will be happy." He brought Europe to her knees. He made thousands of widows and orphans, but he died a broken man in exile. I would not say that his life counted. But during the Civil War a man was picked up off the battlefield in North Georgia. No one thought that he would live, but he promised God that if He would permit him to live, he would give his life to the cause of Christ. The years went by and when this great man died he left a church in Philadelphia which he had founded, a large university, and two great hospitals. Russell Conwell's life counted, because Christ was the center of it.

I pick up a little acorn and it says to me, "One day I will be a great tree. The birds will nest in my boughs and men will rest beneath my shade. I will furnish ribs for mighty ships and provide a warm fireside and a roof overhead for loving families." And I say, "Little acorn, are you going to do all of this?" And the acorn says, "Yes, God and I will do it." And a man says to me, "I want my life to count for others. I want blessings to flow out from my life to many people." And 1 say to him, "Can you

The Hope of the World

do this?" And he says, "Yes, God and I together can do it." So if you want your life to count, just link it to God.

4. *Another question — what about the future life?* Long ago, a man asked, "If a man die shall he live again?" And Jesus over and over says, "Don't fear the future. Just trust Me. I am out there in the future and I will care for you." A Christian doctor was visiting one of his patients who was quite ill. The man said, "Doctor, will I get well?" And the doctor replied, "I am afraid not." The man then said, "I fear death. Can you tell me what is on the other side of the grave?" The doctor frankly said, "No, I cannot tell you all that is beyond the door of death." Just about that time the door opened, and the doctor's dog ran in and leaped up on him and loved him. The doctor then turned to the sick man and said, "You see, my dog had never been in here, but he knew that his master was here, so he came in without fear. I cannot tell you what is on the other side of the door of death, but I know this, our Master is there and that is enough. You just trust Him and when the door opens, you can enter without fear."

On Staten Island in New York harbor they have a home for old seamen, called "Snug Harbor." When the sailors are too old to serve and too poor to live elsewhere, they come to live in this rest home. Oh, because of Jesus, there is a Snug Harbor waiting for us at the end of the way!

During the Franco-Prussian War a young lieutenant marched away to battle. He told the girl that he loved good-by, promising to come back and marry her and provide a home for her. When the war was over and the troops came marching home, the girl looked in vain for her lover. But he had been killed in battle. She would not believe this, but she kept on saying, "But he must come. He must come." The poor girl lost her reason and through the years until she died, she came to the gate each day to wait for her beloved.

She was greatly disappointed, but let me tell you that Jesus never disappoints. He will take away your sins if you come to Him now. He will walk with you down the pathway of life. He will provide a home for you at the end of the way. He is my hope — He is your hope — He is the world's hope for time and eternity.

Sermon 9

CHRIST AND THE HOME

Joshua 24:14-24

The first institution ever built by God or man was the home. Not the church, as important as it is. Not an orphanage or hospital or home for the aged, not a school or university. The first institution was the home and it was built by God Himself. He created Adam and put him in the Garden of Eden. This must have been the most beautiful place that ever existed. It was fresh from the hand of God and filled with all that was good and pleasant. But Adam was lonely. He needed what every man needs — the love and companionship of a good woman. So God put him to sleep and performed an operation upon him. When Adam awakened, he saw before him the most beautiful creature his eyes had ever looked upon. He fell in love with her at first sight and God united them in marriage in the Garden of Eden.

That was the first home. Since that time it has been God's plan for men and women to leave their old homes, to become united in holy wedlock, and to set up homes of their own. Now that home may be a mansion or a cottage, it may be an apartment or a tent. But if two people live there, bound together by the cords of love, it is a home.

In the last few years we have had a great building boom in America. Hundreds of new subdivisions have been opened up and thousands of new homes have been built. But there has been a serious shortage in another direction. We're building many houses but very few Christian homes. Yet I tell you that if America is to stand, everything good that we have must be founded on the Christian home. When you start to build a house, you pick out the kind of foundation that you want. Then you pick out your walls and then you pick out the roof. Let us do the same thing as we think of building a Christian home.

I. The Foundation Should Be Faith

As we read the text we hear Joshua in his farewell message to Israel. He reminds the people of the goodness of God toward them. Then he calls upon them to forsake all other gods and to follow Jehovah. "But," he says, "regardless of what *you* do, as for me and my house, we will serve the Lord." Now that must be the decision of everyone who wants to build a Christian home. You must lay a foundation of faith in Christ and only then are you ready to build. The pitiful thing today is that so many people are building their homes upon a rotten foundation. They build upon worldliness and sin and booze and beer and complete forgetfulness of God.

On April 10, 1852, an American citizen died in Algiers and was buried in Tunis. Thirty-one years later the United States Government sent a war ship to bring this man's body back home. As the ship drew near New York, great crowds went out to meet him. The bands played patriotic music, the guns thundered out a welcome. All flags flew at half mast. A special train bore the body to Washington. Congress adjourned and the president and all the high officials stood with uncovered heads as the funeral procession moved down Pennsylvania Avenue. Who was that man? What great battle had he fought? None. What great book had he written? None. What great oration had he delivered? None. What great picture had he painted? None. What great invention had he perfected? None. What had he done? He had written a song — a song which touched the hearts of millions of people. The man was John Howard Payne. He wrote "Home Sweet Home." But no home can be called that unless it is founded on Christ. Is He the foundation stone of your home? Are you building your home and rearing your children on Christ the Solid Rock?

A beautiful young woman married a wealthy man. Neither of them was a Christian. They reared several children. But the name of God was never mentioned in that home except in profanity. Prayer was never offered, the Bible was never read, the blessing was never asked at the table, and none of the family ever went to church. After the children grew up and were married, the father died. The mother went to church at last, seeking comfort. She found Christ as her Saviour and He became everything to her. But one day she came weeping to her pastor. She said, "We built our home and reared our children without Christ. We had no Bible reading, no prayer, no church life. Now I have found Christ and I have gone to my children and asked them to come to church and serve the Lord. But they only laugh at me. Oh, what a mistake I made when I did not build my home upon Christ!" Some of you are making the same mistake. You are putting the world first. Christ and the church have a small place in your lives. Some day your children will break your hearts and as you sit in sorrow you will have to say, "I had it coming to me."

I have seen both kinds of homes — the home where Christ was honored and the home where He was ignored. Oh, what a difference there is between the two. This difference can be seen now, but it can be seen more clearly in the results that will come in after years. I have seen scores of homes and families go on the rocks because God didn't have a place in those homes. On the other hand, I have seen many homes of happiness and usefulness because God had a place in those homes. So I urge you to build your home on Christ. This is the strongest foundation that you can lay. The storms of life can never wreck this home. Be sure that Christ is your rock and your salvation.

II. THE WALLS OF THE HOME

1. *The first wall is that of consecrated Christian living.* Having founded the home on Christ, you must continue daily to live a consecrated life for Him. I often see the motto in homes, "CHRIST IS THE HEAD OF THIS HOME, THE UNSEEN GUEST AT EVERY MEAL, THE UNSEEN LISTENER TO EVERY CONVERSATION." This is not enough unless the children can see Christ in their mothers and fathers.

There are two ways to teach children — by precept and by example. First, by telling them what to do, then by doing it yourself. And an ounce of example is worth a ton of teaching. A preacher friend tells about staying in a certain home during a revival. One day the father beat one of the boys unmercifully for smoking, yet every day the father himself sat around puffing on a pipe. When the preacher reminded this man of his influence, the man said, "I have smoked all my life, but God helping me, I don't intend for my boys to smoke if I have to beat the life out of them." This father was failing in his influence.

Oh, mothers and fathers, what kind of an example are you setting? Drinking that cocktail and guzzling that beer and doing certain other things may seem very little in your sight. But think of the example you are setting. You may unknowingly lead your children into pathways that will ruin them. I know many parents who are not living as they should for God. They may be saved, but Christ does not have the first place in their lives. They are neglecting their simple Christian duties and thus setting a bad example. I know its harder to go to church and tithe and keep up religion in the home than simply to let go. But it really pays off in the long run.

Recently a man said, "The saddest day of my life was when I moved to the city. Back in the small town my family always went to church and lived for the Lord. But since we came to the city we have given our time to the things that are frivolous and foolish and futile. The saddest day of my life was when we moved to the city." And the saddest day of any man's life is when he begins to put the things of the world before the things of God. The first wall of the house, then, is consecrated, dedicated Christian living.

2. *The second wall is composed of the Bible and prayer.* The Bible ought to have a prominent place in every home. Christians realize that, so they buy a Bible and put it in a prominent place in the home. Then they forget that it is there. How many times have your children seen you reading the Bible? Certainly you would rather for them to remember your having a Bible in your hand than a cocktail glass.

And how many times have your children heard you pray? Yes, you learned a little blessing and they hear you say it three times a day at the table. But how many times have they heard you pray from the heart? A preacher visited a member of his church and urged him to have a family altar in the home. Sometime later this man came into the preacher's study and burst into tears. He said, "My little girl died suddenly this morning. I believe that she has gone to be with God, but here is the thing that breaks my heart. She must tell God that she never heard a prayer in her father's house or from her father's lips. Oh, I wish that I had her with me for just one more day."

Yes, we ought to make room for God's word and for prayer in our homes. The child that is brought up in this atmosphere never forgets it.

3. *Another wall in the home is the wall of discipline.* I don't mean cruelty, but I do mean correction in love. We are so lax on this point today. It is much easier to let things slide than to say, "No." Some of the modern psychologists have been steering parents down the wrong road. They say that you must never

deny a child anything, for that might dwarf their little characters. But there is a little of Satan in all of us when we are born. If we fail to discipline our children, we will soon have a "hellion" on our hands. Then they will develop into juvenile delinquents and later on into criminals.

A young woman was telling an older woman about the trouble she was having with her little boy. He was always running away. She said, "As soon as he was able to walk, he would push the gate open and run out into the street. We put a latch on the gate but he soon learned to open it. We put the latch up higher and he would get on a box and open the gate. We put the latch still higher and he learned to open the gate with a stick. I just don't know what to do." The older and wiser woman said, "Why don't you put the latch on the boy?" She was simply saying, "Use some discipline with the boy and you won't have to worry about his running away."

What is the purpose of discipline? Simply to make us better. If a father punishes a child, it isn't because he hates him, it is because he loves him and wants to help build his character. The Bible says, "Whom the Lord loveth He chasteneth." It also tells us that discipline is not pleasant, but it brings a rich reward. If you love your children, exercise some discipline with them and one day they will thank you for it.

4. *Another wall is the wall of reverence.* We need to teach our children to have reverence for certain things.

First, we should teach reverence for God. We must never use His Name in the wrong way. I often hear people use the expression, "My God!" This is not honoring God and not pleasing to Him and it sounds very cheap. Let me tell you what came out in a recent paper. Piper Laurie of Hollywood, in describing a visit to Korea, said, "I felt just wonderful because I knew that there were not four of us, but five of us in that jeep. And guess who the fifth passenger was? It was good old God." Jane Russell who has prayer meetings in her back yard, said, "I love God. When you get to know Him, you will find that He is a living doll." Tallulah Bankhead, on the Jack Paar show, said "I talk to that cat, Jesus Christ, every night." Sounds awful, doesn't it? And it is. We must teach our children a deeper reverence for God than that.

Then we must teach reverence for God's Day. Sunday ought to be different from other days. It is God's day and not ours. We have no right to use it for ourselves. The President was criticized for having a cocktail party on Sunday night. But that is no worse than some of you who think Sunday is the time to go visiting or fishing or to some sports or entertainment event.

Too many parents let their children do as they please about going to church. We never had any trouble along these lines with our boys. It was just a settled fact that on Sunday we would go to church, so there was no question about it. Church-going on Sunday was just as much a habit as going to school on Monday. Don't let anything keep you from church. When Uncle Bob or Aunt Susie come visiting you, invite them to come to church with you. If they won't come, let them sit at home alone. You may get rid of some unwelcome relatives that way. Don't let anybody rob you of the spiritual blessings of worship.

Then we must teach reverence for God's house. The church is no place for children to run around in as if it were a gymnasium. It is not a place for laughter and talk. While we rejoice in the freedom that we have and the sweet fellowship that we enjoy, I do plead for more reverence. I would like to see us get back to the old-fashioned idea of families sitting together. Often I see parents sitting near their children while their children misbehave during the service and yet the parents pay no attention to it.

This also means reverence for church property. We have no right to mutilate anything in the church or to waste anything. It has been bought with sacred money and we ought to respect it.

Then we must teach reverence for parents. The children should never refer to the "old man" or the "old lady." Of course, parents ought so to live as to command respect from the children. God says, "Honour thy father and thy mother." The children can't honor the parents if they are not the right kind of people.

Now we have the four walls of the home. We have consecrated Christian living, Bible reading and prayer, discipline, and reverential respect.

III. The Roof Is Love, Covering Everything

Troubles may come, financial disaster may strike, and sorrow may break the heart. But if those who live in the home love each other, they will weather the storm. I remember a picture from my childhood. It was that of a dear old couple sitting by the fireside. They gazed into the flames and thought of all the years they had spent together and the trials they had endured. Yet you could see the glow of contentment and happiness on their faces, because love had brought them through and still sustained them.

Now there must be a mutual love in the home. It must never be one-sided. The husband is to love the wife and the wife is to love the husband. Parents are to love the children, and the children are to love the parents. This is the roof that must cover the home and bring happiness to all who live there. Napoleon said, "The greatest need of France is for more Christian homes." That's the need of America today. You can't decide for other homes, but from this day forward you can decide that yours will be a Christian home.

In the olden days a doctor was called one night to drive eight miles out into the country to see a patient who was seriously ill. The snow was falling heavily and he knew that he could not find the way to that house without some help. So he phoned the people in the first house and told them to put a light in the window. Then he asked them to phone the next house and have them to put a light in their window. Soon there was a string of lights reaching all the way out to the sick man's home. The doctor was able to find his way through the snow and the darkness.

This is what our homes ought to be. They ought to be lights along the highway leading to God and heaven. God help us to keep the light of a Christian home forever burning brightly.

Sermon 10

THE TEACHINGS OF CHRIST APPLIED TO MODERN LIFE
(Part One)

Luke 7:24-29

Someone has said that "a university is Mark Hopkins on one end of the log and a boy on the other end." They were simply saying that it takes a great teacher to make a great school. The schools that have blessed the world were not made by physical equipment, nor were they made by large endowments, nor were they made by winning football teams. A good school is made by the right kind of teachers. The president of one of our fine Christian colleges was attending a banquet in a northern state. He was talking to another college president about the matter of making the school thoroughly Christian. This president said to him, "How can we make our school a Christian school? Must we change the curriculum?" And the first president answered, "No, mathematics, language, and science are the same everywhere. In order to have a Christian school, we must have Christian teachers to teach these subjects."

Now if a great school is made by great teachers, you and I go to the best school in the world. We pay no entrance fee, we take no examination, we don't even have to leave home. Jesus is the Master Teacher. You and I can sit at His feet and learn the most important lessons of life. He towers above all other teachers as the mountain towers above a molehill. "He spake as never a man spake before." Those who heard Him were amazed and exclaimed, "He speaks as one having authority and not as a scribe."

Suppose that Jesus came today to our land. What would He teach? He would teach a great many things and in these two sermons I would like to tell you about a few of these things.

I. First, the Primary Thing Is to Establish Right Relationship With God

When the lawyer asked Jesus to tell him which was the great commandment, Jesus replied, "Thou shalt love the Lord thy God with all thine heart and soul and mind and strength." Now how can we establish this relationship?

1. *We are to come to God through His Son.* This is God's plan. In the olden days God seemed high above and far away. But in Jesus God bent down and made a way of approach to the Heavenly Father. Jesus Himself said, "No man cometh unto the Father but by me. I am the way, the truth and the life."

Peter Cartright, a bold Methodist preacher of another day, was preaching in the city of Nashville. General Andrew Jackson entered the church just before Cartright rose to preach. The pastor whispered to Cartright, saying, "Be careful what you say. General Jackson is in the congregation." When Cartright arose to preach he said, "Your pastor tells me that General Jackson is in the congregation. What does that matter? If he doesn't repent of his sins and trust Jesus Christ as his Saviour, he will be damned when he dies just like any other sinner." Later Jackson congratulated the preacher on his courage. Cartright was simply saying that all who come to God must come the same way.

Sin stands between man and God. Man is never in right relationship to God until he climbs over that sin. And there is no way to do it except through Christ. What a happy day that was! Do you remember it? You were living in sin, you had no peace in your heart, your guilt seemed too heavy to bear. Then you looked up and saw a Man on the cross. You knew that He loved you, you knew He was dying for you, you knew that He was inviting you to come to Him. Through your tears you went to Him, you fell at the foot of the cross, and He threw His arms around you and saved you. Now you can sing of a wonderful Saviour who has redeemed you, who walks with you and who is taking you to heaven.

2. *We are to surrender to Him as Lord.* Too many people are content just to have their sins forgiven. But Jesus came not only to be our Saviour but to be our Lord. However, He is a gentleman. He will not force His way into your heart. You must invite Him. The tragedy of millions today is that they say they believe in Him, but they don't let Him into their lives as Lord. Yet I wonder if you are really saved when Jesus means no more than simply a fire escape for you.

Oh, after all that He has done for you and all that He means to you, how can you go on living as if He never lived and never died? Let's open up our hearts and say, "Come in, Lord Jesus. Sit upon the throne of my heart. Rule me, guide me, fill me.

Take charge of my personal life, my business life, my home life. Rule every part of me."

3. *We are to strive to please Him in all things.* Why does a man work and slave for years to give things to his wife and children? It is because he loves them. If we love Jesus we will spend our years trying to please Him. Paul always tried to please Christ. For Him he gave up all things and counted nothing dear to himself. He walked the way of suffering and death. And when you ask him how he was able to do all of these things, he replies, "The love of Christ constrains me."

So Jesus would teach today that the most important thing in life is to get right with God. This is more important than money. More important than health, more important than education, more important than anything. Have you learned your lesson? Is your heart right with God?

II. Next, He Would Teach Us to Establish Right Relationships With Our Fellowman

This naturally follows. If we are completely right with God, we will get right with man. If we are not treating others rightly, we are not in tune with God.

1. *This means that we are to love all men.* Jesus loved them, no matter what their station in life. So should we love them. Of course, it is natural that we will love some more than others, but we are not to hate anyone. As a cancer eats away the physical life, so does hatred eat away the spiritual life.

2. *This means that we are to have the right spirit toward all men.* His was a spirit of love and forgiveness. Do you have it? When asked how many times we should forgive one another, He replied, "Seventy times seven." That is four hundred and ninety times. Can you forgive that often? Again He said, "If you forgive not men their trespasses, neither can God forgive you your trespasses." That's serious business. A bishop and a nobleman exchanged some bitter words and parted in anger. Late that afternoon the bishop remembered that the Bible said, "Let not the sun go down upon your wrath." He sent a messenger to the nobleman to say, "My Lord, the sun is going down." They soon came together and were reconciled. It is a good rule not to let the sun go down on your anger. You will sleep better at night if you get these bitter things out of your heart.

Sometimes we hear someone say, "I am going to get even with him if it is the last thing I do." Well, that ought to be the last thing that you try to do. That is Satanic philosophy. God says, "Vengeance is mine, *I* will repay." It is not our place to get even — it is our place to be Christ-like. Whatever anyone else does or says, we must act as Christians. Often we may be casting our pearls before swine and our good intentions may prove useless, but if we have done our part we can rest easy at night.

Some years ago I felt that a certain man was angry with me. I wrote him the sweetest letter that it was possible for me to write, asking for his forgiveness and love. He never answered the letter. I felt that if anyone had written me a letter like that, no mode of communication in the world would have been fast enough to carry to him my message of love and forgiveness. Oh, as a Christian, never let it be said of you that you hate anyone!

3. *This means that we are to encourage others.* A soldier was telling how he was wounded in battle and someone asked him, "Did you fall at once?" He replied, "No, the other men saw that I was wounded and they gathered around so close that I couldn't fall." Now that's real brotherhood. And our comrades on the road of life are often hurt and wounded. We must not let them down. We must not forsake them when they fall. They need our help. So check up on yourself. How do you stand in your relationship to others? If there is anything between you and anyone else, be a Christian and get it out. Jesus said, "Therefore, all things whatsoever ye would that men should do to you, do ye even so to them."

III. THEN JESUS WOULD TEACH US THAT IT IS MORE IMPORTANT TO GAIN ETERNAL THINGS THAN TEMPORAL THINGS

He told us to lay up our treasures in heaven, not upon the earth. Is He saying that we ought not to make any provisions for the future? No. He is saying that it is wrong to lay aside all of our treasures upon this earth and send nothing up to heaven. I have known rich men who spent a lifetime piling up wealth. Then they died and left it all behind and went up before God empty-handed. This is sinful.

An old preacher was praying and he said, "Lord, help us to trust our souls to Thee." This request was followed by a chorus of "Amens." Then he prayed, "Lord, help us to trust our bodies to Thee." Again there were many "Amens." Next he prayed, "Lord, help us to trust our money to Thee." Everything was quiet; there were no "Amens." Yes, many people are willing to trust God to save them and give them good health, but they don't want to trust Him with their money.

He told us that life did not consist in the abundance of things which we possess. This is certainly true. Many people who have little are happier than those who have much. "Things" cannot bring happiness. You must have something else on the inside. If you are sad, can "things" make you glad? If you are hurt, can "things" heal a broken heart? If you are troubled, can "things" guide you to the light? No. You must have the Holy Spirit within you to help you in every time of need. The Bible tells us that the things which we see are temporal, while the eternal things are those things which are unseen.

David Garrick took Dr. Samuel Johnson to see a fine home in Hampton Court. Dr. Johnson looked at the garden, the statues, and the pictures. Garrick expected him to compliment these things. But he said, "Ah, David, David, these are the things that make a deathbed terrible!" If you love the things that you see too much, you will lose your love for the things that you can't see.

Three men were talking together after the Chicago fire. One man said, "Thank God, there are some things which fire cannot burn." He could say that because just the year before he had given away a million dollars to the cause of Christ. All that he had saved was what he had given away. It was up in heaven where fire couldn't touch it. If Jesus were here today, I believe He would say, "Quit giving all of your time and energy and thought to material things. Get busy for Me. Serve Me and My church and day by day you will be laying up treasures in heaven."

IV. THEN HE WOULD TEACH THAT HIS BUSINESS IS THE GREATEST BUSINESS IN THE WORLD

Standard Oil is big business, General Motors is big business, United States Steel is big business. But the greatest business of all is that of the Lord Jesus Christ. When all other business has failed, His will still be going on.

1. *His business affects the world more than any other business.* When you buy an automobile, what does that mean? It means a few years of transportation and the employment of a few people. But when a soul is saved, it means that a life is changed and an eternity is changed from hell to heaven. When you do things for God, you set influences in motion that will last forever. It is like throwing a rock into a lake. The circles in

the water will reach to the farthest shore. And when you do something for God, that influence reaches to the shores of eternity.

2. *Then His business pays the biggest dividends.* A man invests his money in a good stock and once a quarter he receives a dividend. But he who invests in God's business reaps eternal dividends. Judson invested his life in Burma and the dividends continue even though he has been dead for many years. Livingston invested his life in Africa, and that investment is still paying big dividends. Billy Graham is investing his life all over the world, and the dividends will be eternal. You may not be able to make such heavy investments, but you can do what you can and it will pay dividends.

I held a meeting in Atlanta some years ago, and the Lord blessed with many conversions. Three years later I saw the chairman of the deacons of that church. He said to me, "Do you remember Mr. So-and-so? He was saved during your meeting. He has grown greatly as a Christian and has been ordained as a deacon. If the meeting produced no other results, it was certainly worthwhile." That was my dividend, coming three years later.

Here is one of the greatest promises in the Bible. "Seek ye first the kingdom of God and his righteousness, and all these things shall be added unto you." Christ was simply saying, "Invest your life with Me, and you will receive dividends here and hereafter."

3. *His business is the most enduring in the world.* You look back over the years and you see many changes in every city. Businesses which once were strong exist no more. Banks which once were a bulwark of safety have closed their doors. But God's business never fails. It has been going on for years, and it grows stronger all the while. So if you will line up in God's business, you will never fail. Moody's tomb has this inscription upon it, "He that doeth the will of God abideth forever." Our earthly deeds will perish, but what we do for God will abide forever.

Here is another promise. Those who look after God's business have the promise of His presence. He said, "Lo, I will be with you alway." What a wonderful promise! David Livingston spent many years in Africa. He then came back to Glasgow to receive a degree from the university. As he stood to speak, one arm hung limply by his side. He had been attacked by lions. He told of the hardships of his work and his plans for the future. Then he said, "Shall I tell you what supported me all the years among the people whose language was strange, and who were often hostile to my work? It was the promise of Christ, 'Lo, I will be with you alway.'" God's presence gives us strength. As you and I follow Him, we can be assured that He is always near.

So listen to Jesus as He teaches in these modern times. He tells us to get into right relationship with God. He tells us to get into right relationship with our fellow man. He tells us to put eternal things above temporal things. He tells us to get lined up in the biggest business in the world.

Moses died just before the children of Israel crossed over Jordan into the Promised Land. Joshua was given command. A tremendous burden fell upon him. But God spoke to him and said, "Be strong and of good courage. As I was with Moses, so will I be with you." With that promise in his heart he faced the men of Israel and said to them, "Will you leave your homes, your loved ones, your cattle, to help us to conquer Canaan?" And they gave him this answer, "All that thou commandeth us, we will do, and whithersoever thou sendeth us we will go."

That was beautiful obedience. Oh, that we had the same spirit today! Our Leader is greater than Joshua. He calls us to serve Him and the world. Let us say, "Here am I, Lord, Take me and use me. Where you send, I will go, and what you command, I will do."

Sermon 11

THE TEACHINGS OF CHRIST APPLIED TO MODERN LIFE
(Part Two)

Matthew 11:25-30

In my first sermon on this subject, I said that if Jesus were here today He would teach four things. First, the primary thing is to get into the right relationship with God. Second, we are then to get into right relationship with man. Third, eternal things are more important than temporal things, and fourth, we should line up in the biggest business in the world, God's business.

The character of a man's teaching is measured by the after-lives of his pupils. Before World War I Germany had many great universities. The scholars of America felt that they had not received a complete education until they had received a Ph.D. degree from one of these universities. Now these schools were materialistic, skeptical, modernistic, and atheistic in their teachings. This philosophy brought on the war, the philosophy that "might is right." The Germans felt that it was perfectly all right to kill people and ravage nations to gain their ends. God was entirely forgotten.

When the American scholars returned to our country, a wave of modernism soon filled America. The schools were saturated with new thought, unbelief, and skepticism. These ideas soon reached into some of the pulpits of the land. Many universities, which for many years had been lighthouses for God's truth, broke their moorings and were swept out into the whirlpools of doubt and unbelief. Our country has suffered ever since because of the wrong kind of teachers. The teacher is the thing that counts in a school. A Christian teacher will seek to send out Christian students. An atheistic teacher will seek to turn out atheistic students. The teacher makes the pupil.

Do you want to see the kind of teacher that Jesus was? Then look at His pupils. They went out to give their lives away for the Gospel and Christ. It was said of them that they "turned the

The Teachings of Christ Applied to Modern Life 91

world upside down." Again it was said of them, "See how they love one another!" They had not only learned the great lessons of life from Jesus, but they had caught His spirit. One philosopher has said, "Jesus did more to soften and regenerate humanity than all the philosophers and all the teachers that have lived since the world began."

When you read the list of men who have blessed the world, you find that they were men who had learned great lessons at the feet of Jesus. With few exceptions, the great humanitarians, the great philosophers, and the great scientists were men of God. Through the ages they sat at the feet of Jesus and learned of Him. Now Jesus is still teaching. Let us now think of some other things which He would teach if He were here today.

I. He Would Teach That the Internal Things of the Spirit Count More Than the External Things

The majority of people feel today that the chief aim in life is to gain the external things. So they spend their money, time and talent on material things. A man wants a good home, two automobiles, two TV sets, and security in his old age. There is nothing wrong with this desire. These things are not necessarily evil things. But often a man gives up the best in order to gain the good. Here is a man wrapped up in his business. He gives it his very best. That is all right, but not if his business keeps him from going to church and serving God. Here is a woman who has a beautiful home. She wants to keep it spotless and comfortable. That is all right, but it is wrong if she is such a slave to the home that she has no time to serve God. Here is a young man who wants to get an education. It is perfectly all right for one to prepare himself for his life's work, but this is wrong if it stifles his spiritual life. Many people are doing things which are all right in themselves, but they are just not the best things. God wants you to enjoy life, but your spiritual responsibility comes first. Anything that comes between you and God is wrong.

What are some of the important internal things? Well, there is peace with God. Isn't it better to have that than material things? Is there anything better than knowing that your sins have been forgiven, and that you have the right relationship toward God? Then what about a sense of Divine fellowship? Isn't it wonderful just to know that you are God's child and that He cares for you, that He walks with you day by day, helping you out in every time of need? Then there are the graces mentioned in the Bible. "The fruit of the spirit is love, joy, peace, longsuffering, gentleness, goodness, faith, meekness, temperance." These things are worth more than silver and gold. Yes, if Jesus were here, I believe He would say, "I want you to have all the comforts and conveniences of life, but these inner spiritual things bring far more personal satisfaction. I want you to have them, too."

II. Next, He Would Teach That Anxiety Is Sinful and Needless

Anxiety is sinful because it shows that we don't trust Him. If we trust Him, we don't worry; if we worry, we don't trust. When we think of all that He said about caring for us, can't we trust Him?

Jesus said, "Behold the fowls of the air: they sow not, neither do they reap, nor gather into barns; yet your heavenly Father feedeth them." He also said, "Consider the lilies of the field, how they grow, they toil not, neither do they spin. And yet I say unto you, that Solomon in all of his glory was not arrayed like one of these." He said that God took note of the sparrow's fall and that we are worth more than many sparrows. He said that He would be with us until the end of the way, that He would never leave us nor forsake us. In view of all of these promises, isn't it sinful when we don't trust Him? Yet when troubles come we fly into the face of God and say, "I don't know why this had to come to me. This is too much." By such an attitude we do not please the God who promises to care for those who trust Him. We need to learn to practice the presence of God. He is not far off — He is a close friend. He is interested in everything about us.

We sing the song, "The arm of flesh will fail you, you dare not trust your own." How true this is. We cannot trust ourselves, but we can trust the mighty arm of God.

Anxiety is not only sinful, it is needless. When I was growing up I wanted to be very tall. Then I read in the Bible that no one could add anything to his height by worry. That settled the matter. Worry aggravates a problem. It does not help you out of your difficulty. When you are in debt, when you lose your job, when troubles come your way and people are mistreating you, do not say, "I will sit down and worry about these things. Everything will be better." No, they will only get worse. It is up to us to do our dead level best and ask God to take care of the rest.

The Teachings of Christ Applied to Modern Life 93

One dark night a man fell into a steep place. On the way down he caught hold of a bush and held fast. Soon his strength began to ebb and he knew that he would soon fall down to his death. But when his strength gave out and he did fall, he fell only twelve inches, and landed on solid ground. Some of us are like that. We worry and struggle when what we need to do is simply to turn loose and fall into the "everlasting arms." Yes, Jesus would teach us that we are to trust more and worry less.

III. Then He Would Teach Us That a Man May Be Down, But He Is Never Out

Look at Simon Peter weeping against the wall. If ever a man felt that it was all over, he did. But Jesus gave him one look of love and forgiveness and he went out to become a great servant of the Lord. If he had quit, his name would have gone down in shame. He was down, but he didn't take the full count. He followed Christ and came out all right.

On New Year's Day of 1928 I listened to the broadcast of the Rose Bowl Game when Georgia Tech was playing California. Suddenly the announcer cried out, "Reigals has the ball and is running the wrong way!" In the scramble of play he had scooped up the ball, had lost sense of direction, and was running toward Tech's goal line. One of his comrades tackled him just before he made a touchdown for the opposing team. He was saddened and humiliated by this experience. During the half he sat in a corner of the dressing room, weeping and crying out that he didn't want to live. But his coach, Nibs Price, said to him, "Roy, the game is just one half over. I want you to go back in there and give it your best." Roy never forgot those words. We also make mistakes. We often run the wrong way, but our Great Coach always gives us another chance. The devil does get us down; he gets his feet on our neck, but we don't have to stay down. We can reach out a hand to Jesus and He will help us up and give us a new start.

IV. Then He Would Teach That Happiness Comes From Service and Not From Selfishness.

There is an old story which tells us that Death came to a man when that man was twenty years of age. He said to the man, "Come with me." But the man replied, "Not yet. Please let me learn the meaning of life first." Death then promised to give him another twenty years. He came back when the man was forty.

He came back when the man was sixty and the man had not yet learned the true meaning of life. When Death came back for him at eighty and took him away, he still declared that he had not learned the true meaning of life. But Jesus says, "Life is a span of years given to us to be used to glorify God, to help others, and to make the world a better place in which to live."

During the Civil War a Christian soldier was imprisoned. Three times he was offered his freedom and each time he declined that freedom in order for a sick soldier to go free in his place. Then his fourth opportunity came. He had been trying to win another prisoner to Christ, but the man said, "I do not believe in religion. I have seen no evidences of it." Then the Christian man elected to stay in prison in order that this man might go free. This man was so impressed by this act of kindness and sacrifice that all of his excuses were broken down and he was saved. The Christian soldier had learned the true meaning of life. If more of us would show forth Christ in unselfish service, our lives would count more for Him. Yes, if Jesus were here today, He would say as He did nineteen hundred years ago, "He that would find his life, must lose it for my sake." The way of real happiness is the way of service to others in the Name of Christ.

V. Then He Would Teach That the Praise of God Is Rather
    to Be Sought Than the Praise of Man.

Do you hold some position in the work of Christ? Are you working for the glory of God or for the praise of men? Some workers are very faithful and active as long as they have that praise, but they quit cold when the shouting dies. Jesus set a good example for us in this respect. When people said good things about Him, it did not turn His head. When they said evil things about Him, this did not affect Him. He was listening for another voice and one day it came. God said, "This is my beloved Son in whom I am well pleased." If He were here today, He would say, "The praise that comes from above is sweeter than all the world. Work for that praise and let nothing turn you aside from it."

VI. Then He Would Teach Us to Loosen Our Grip Upon
    Temporal Things and Hold Fast to the Things
        Which Endure Forever.

He would tell us to give more time and thought and money to the things of God and less time to the things which die with

The Teachings of Christ Applied to Modern Life

the setting sun. Oh, so many of our church people think that the greatest reward of life is to rise high in worldly circles and to get their name in the public eye. They are giving their lives to the things which do not count for God and for which there is no reward in heaven. If Jesus were here today I am sure that He would say, "These things don't count with God. I gave My life for His kingdom. . . . I died for people. Give your life for these things, the things which help people to know the way of eternal life."

Jesus told the story of a certain man who had a big farm. One year he had such wonderful crops that he had to tear down his smaller barns and build larger ones. His bank account was bigger than ever. He had everything. He was going to live a full life and enjoy all of his earthly goods. Then his poor starved soul asked, "What about me? I can't live on big crops and full bank accounts." And the man said, "Take it easy, soul. Eat, drink and be merry." That night the man lay down to sleep on his downy couch and in the middle of the night Death came stalking into the room, saying, "You will not live to enjoy the fruits of your labor. Come with me." And the poor rich man had to turn loose his possessions and go out into a world where those earthly things did not count. Oh, let's loosen our hold now upon the world and take a sure and firm grip upon the things of God!

A well-known opera singer went to a small town for her vacation. She knew that she had some important mail coming and went down to the post office to get this registered mail. The postmaster said, "I am sorry, but I can't give you this mail unless you can present positive means of identification." She showed him her credit cards, but he said, "I am sorry, but this is not enough. Sometimes the credit cards are lost and someone else uses them." The singer thought for just a moment and then she said to herself, *I know what I'll do. I'll sing.* She began to sing in her rich, full, wonderful voice, and soon the little post office was crowded with people. She held them spellbound during the song, then she asked, "Now, may I have my mail?" And the postmaster said, "Yes, I know that you are the great opera singer. I have your records in my home." She identified herself by her singing. How can we identify ourselves? How can we prove to the world that we are Christians? We can do this simply by applying His teachings and showing His Spirit in all things.

So the Great Teacher stands before us and teaches us the

finest lessons of life. Are you willing to learn those lessons? Are you willing to put them into practice? Now if you follow the Great Teacher, someday you will graduate. On that commencement day you will meet Him and hear Him say, "You have fought a good fight, you have been faithful to Me. Well done. Enter into the joys of thy Lord." Oh, what a day that will be!

In the Military Manual of the United States Army the different battles are described. Then the manual tells us why these battles were won or lost. In one of the battles of the Civil War, the South was victorious. Then the question was asked, "Why did the North lose? She had more men and more ammunition." And the simple answer is given, "But the South had General Lee." The forces of the world are greater than we are. If we fight alone we are sure to be defeated. But we have a great Leader, the Lord Jesus Christ. So let's follow Him and His teachings and the victory is sure to be ours.

Sermon 12

IF JESUS CAME BACK TOMORROW

I Thessalonians 4:13-18

As we look back over the centuries we see that some tremendous things have happened. It was a great day when God created the world and all that is in it. It was a great but sad day when man went down into sin, bringing the human race down with him. It was a great day when the Flood came to destroy the earth. It was a great day when David became Israel's greatest king. It was a great day when Paul was saved. It was a great day when America was discovered. It was a great day when Martin Luther challenged the ecclesiastical authorities and brought on the Reformation. But the greatest day of all the past was when Jesus came into the world to die for our sins and to bring salvation within the reach of every man.

Yes, that's the greatest event of the past, and the greatest event of the future will be his coming again. I do not need to refresh your minds with Scriptural proof of His coming. All through the New Testament we hear the loud cry, "He is coming again, He is coming again!" Now many prophecies in the Bible tell us of what will happen before He comes. Did you know that all of these prophecies have been fulfilled? Nothing stands today between us and the coming of Christ in the air. He may come any minute — it may be many years distant. But as we look out upon this chaotic world today, it seems that the time is ripe for His coming. Surely nothing but the return of the Lord can straighten out the world today. Now if Jesus came back tomorrow, what would be the results?

I. IF JESUS CAME BACK TOMORROW, MANY PEOPLE WOULD BE GREATLY SURPRISED.

Now throughout the world we know that thousands of Christians are looking for His coming. They know it could happen at any minute. They would not be surprised, they would be overjoyed. But the majority would be greatly surprised. They have neglected the Bible truth of His coming again. Some people simply don't believe that He is coming. It seems too mystical and too other-worldly for them.

Some people laugh at the idea of His coming. When they do this, they are giving us proof that He is coming again. For the Bible says that in the last days there will be scoffers who ridicule the idea. So when men laugh and scoff at the idea of His coming, they are simply fulfilling Scripture and proving the fact that He is coming again. One of our preachers spoke to a group of ministers recently on the Second Coming. A prominent preacher of another faith said to him, "Surely you don't expect us to believe that." He will be surprised when Jesus comes.

But sinners are going to be surprised most of all. They go along without Christ, thinking that they have plenty of time. Then suddenly when Jesus comes and the Christians are taken out of the world, the sinners are going to be surprised and perplexed. When they finally realize what has happened, they will curse themselves for living for this world only and leaving Christ out.

One of our men had been over in Viet Nam for over a year. His wife knew that he would be coming home sometime soon, but she did not know the day. She longed to see him and often talked to her little girl about the time when "Daddy" would return. He learned that he could come home sooner than he had anticipated, so he hopped a plane and started home without wiring his wife. Then one afternoon she heard a car door slam out in front of the house. She looked out the window and there was her husband. He and his wife and the little girl had a happy reunion. That's the way it will be for the Christian when Jesus comes back. We are waiting now and enduring many things which are hard to bear, but one day Jesus will break through the blue and come back to get us. What a wonderful day that will be!

We were surprised when the Japanese bombed Pearl Harbor. We were surprised when the atomic bomb was dropped upon Hiroshima. We were surprised when the Russian major was sent in orbit around the earth. But the greatest surprise the world has ever known will come when Jesus returns.

II. IF JESUS CAME BACK TOMORROW, HE WOULD FIND A GREAT FALLING AWAY FROM THE FAITH.

There was a time when nearly all men believed in God, in the Bible, in the divinity of Christ, in heaven and hell and the judgment. But this is not true today. In the last fifty years modernism and liberalism have crept in and honeycombed many of our religious institutions and even many of our churches. Many men no longer rely on the Bible as truth, but trust in their own wisdom and rely on their own opinions. I am afraid that many preachers today do not believe in such old-fashioned ideas as the depravity of man, salvation through the blood, eternal death, and the other great doctrines. And if the preachers have fallen away that far, what about the average church member?

We see this falling away not only in faith but in practice. Christians are living worldly lives. They are putting the things of the world before the things of Christ. They are putting the institutions and organizations of the world before His church. Any pastor can point to hundreds of people who were once faithful in attendance and living and tithing, but who now never darken the door of the church, never give a cent and live as if they had never heard of Christ. Why is it that only about one half of the church resident membership is present on Sunday morning, one-fifth on Sunday night, and one-sixth on Wednesday night? Why is it that only about one half of our members ever give to the church? I think it is because we are in the last days and there is a wholesale turning away on every hand.

Jesus asked the question in *Luke 18:8* — "When the Son of man cometh, will he find faith on the earth?" He is simply saying that He knows men will be fallen away when He returns. I know a man who used to speak out bitterly against strong drink and worldly evils. He was very active in the church. Today he indulges in all of these things, but he never comes to church. I can multiply that example many fold. That's the falling away which people are doing today. But when Jesus comes, God helping me, I want Him to find me true to His word in doctrine and true to His teachings in practice, living as close to Him as possible.

III. IF JESUS CAME TOMORROW, THE DEAD IN CHRIST WOULD RISE FIRST.

I know something about death. I became acquainted with it when I was four years of age. My mother died on a dark Friday night. Over the years other loved ones have gone on and their bodies have been buried away to await His coming. I have been in scores of homes where my members have died. I have gone to the cemetery hundreds of times and watched a body being lowered into the grave. This is always a sad time, but when Jesus comes in the air, all the bodies of Christians will be raised up to meet Him.

Now when a Christian dies, his body is buried, but his soul goes up to be with God. Then Jesus comes and brings the soul with Him. The body is then raised and soul and body are joined together. Only then will our salvation be complete. Our bodies will undergo a wonderful change as they come out of the grave. The Bible tells us that they will be changed into His own glorious likeness. This means that we shall be perfect physically, spiritually, and mentally.

So if Jesus came tomorrow, the graves would give up the bodies of Christians, the seas would give up the dead which are in them, and the desert sands would surrender their dead. The body of every Christian would be raised. The bodies of the unsaved would remain in their graves for a thousand years.

IV. IF JESUS CAME TOMORROW, ALL LIVING CHRISTIANS WOULD BE CAUGHT UP TO MEET HIM IN THE AIR.

When Jesus comes in the air, some Christians will still be living. What will happen to them? Just as soon as the dead saints are raised up, then all the living Christians will be caught up in a moment to join them and Jesus. And they, too, will be transformed into His likeness that very instant. I wish it could happen this hour. I wish that we could now hear His shout, the voice of the archangel and the trump of God. I wish that He would take us right out of this church and into His presence above. "Oh," you say, "not now! I have many plans for the future. I am going to be happy here on earth." Poor soul! If Jesus came for you this hour, you would find a million times greater happiness at His side. All of your cares and responsibilities would be over, you would have perfect health, and all of your tears would be wiped away.

When John was on the Isle of Patmos Jesus said to him, "Behold I come quickly." And the dear old saint cried out, "Even so, come Lord Jesus." Oh, if we knew all that His coming meant we would cry out the same thing.

Of course, this will mean a great separation. When the Christians go up to meet Jesus, the unsaved will be left in this world to go through the Great Tribulation. They will wonder at first what happened. Then as they miss the Christians and as the world faces chaotic conditions, they will come to realize what has taken place. It will be a sad day for them.

We can imagine a plane flying through the air. The pilot and co-pilot are Christians. When Jesus comes, they will be taken up higher, together with all the passengers who are Christians. No one will be left to fly the plane, and it would crash. The whole world system will be upset when Christians are taken away. Then those who are left will come to realize that Christians are truly "the salt of the earth."

When this separation comes, where are you going to be? Will you be counted with the lost or with the saved? Will you be caught up to meet Jesus or left to face the terrible tribulation period?

V. IF JESUS CAME TOMORROW, ALL OPPORTUNITIES FOR CHRISTIAN SERVICE WOULD BE OVER.

Some of you have been saying, "Someday I am going to settle down. I will quit serving the world and start doing something for Christ." But you may put it off too long. Then when Jesus comes, you will cry out, "Why didn't I give Him my service? Now it is too late."

Somebody said to an Irishman, "Pat, if you had two million dollars, would you give one million to God?" And Pat said, "Sure, if I had two million dollars I would give one million to God." "Well, Pat," they asked, "If you had two farms would you give one of them to God?" And Pat said, "Sure, if I had two farms, I would give one to God." Then one more question was asked, "Well, Pat, if you had two pigs, would you give one to God?" And Pat answered, "Faith, and you knew that I had two pigs before you asked me!" Maybe you can't give big sums to God or render great service, but you can give Him what you have and you can do what you can do for Him.

A young preacher went into the pulpit to preach his first sermon. He thought he had it well prepared. He talked for a few minutes and then stopped. Everything was quiet. After a few minutes he blurted out, "Friends, I am sorry, but I forgot my sermon." As he started to leave the pulpit he heard a voice saying, "Haven't I done anything for you?" "Yes, Lord," he said, "You have done everything." "Well," came the voice, "Couldn't you tell them that?" So he went back to the pulpit and said, "Friends, I see that I can't preach, but I can love Jesus and I want to tell you what He has done for me. You know the wild life that I lived. You know that Christ has made me over. If I can't preach, I am still determined to serve Him all the days of my life."

Oh, you may not do great things for God! But are you doing your best? When He comes, all of your opportunities will be ended.

VI. If Jesus Came Tomorrow, All Your Opportunities to Be Saved Would Be Over

Today God pleads through His Holy Spirit for you to leave your sin and come to Christ. You will not have a chance after He comes. It may be that some will be saved during the Tribulation and the Millenium which follows, but probably none will be saved who have had an opportunity to be saved in this age. Your last chance will come when the trumpet blows and Jesus comes in the air.

A tent meeting was being held in a Texas town. At one of the morning services the preacher asked all those who were saved and ready for the coming of Christ to come to the front and crowd around the big platform. Then he asked the unsaved people to stay in their seats. When this had been done, he sought to explain the separation which would take place when Jesus comes. Those who are unsaved would be forever lost and separated from those who are saved. Some of the members of the same family were at the front and some were still in their seats. The preacher urged those who were unsaved to give their hearts to Christ and to come and join with Christians at the front. The service lasted until one o'clock. Every few minutes someone would come weeping out of their seats and come forward to the platform accepting Christ.

Oh, if Jesus came tomorrow, where would you be? God gives you every opportunity to be saved now, but all of your opportunities will be over when Jesus comes.

VII. If Jesus Came Tomorrow, Then the Tribulation Period Would Begin

I do not have time to tell you all about this period, but the Bible describes it as the worst time the world has ever known. We think we know something of suffering and bloodshed now, but this is nothing to compare with that period. And those who reject Christ will be left down here to suffer all the troubles that will come upon the earth at that time. Christianity and all of its influence will be gone from the earth, but lost men will remember how they ignored the church and rejected every opportunity of salvation. They will cry out for help, but no help will come. The pale horse of death will ride rough-shod through the world and millions will die. And as further suffering comes men will seek death but will not be able to find it.

This is the time when the Antichrist will rule the world. As Christ sought to bring good things to men, so the Antichrist will bring evil things to men. There is only one way to escape this tribulation period. You must come to Christ before it is too late.

Now when will Christ come? No one knows the day nor the hour. But when His body, the Church, is complete, He will come. This means that when the last soul which is to be saved is saved He will return. Colonel Clark, the founder of the Pacific Garden Mission, was there on the job six nights out of every seven. A friend said to him, "Why don't you get some rest? Why don't you take a vacation? You are killing yourself by sticking so close to the Mission." "I can't do that," he replied, "every time that I start to the mission I think that maybe that last man will be saved in our mission tonight and then Jesus would come. I want to be at my post of duty when He comes."

Where are you going to be when He comes, dear friend? Will you be out in the world, away from Christ and His service, or will you be busy for Him? Oh, I tell you, I want Him to find me faithful when He comes.

Dr. H. A. Ironside was doing some missionary work among the Indians. It was before the day of automobiles and he traveled in a wagon. He went out to a service one day and then started to his home base at five o'clock in the afternoon, so that he could be there for the evening service. Soon the sun was gone and the clouds began to boil. They knew that a storm was coming and they were afraid that they would all get caught in it. Then the driver said, "Hold on. I am going to drive fast. I will try to make it to the great rock. If we can get there, we will be safe." He drove hard and Dr. Ironside said that soon they saw a rock fifty feet high rising up from the plain. When the driver came near, he didn't stop. He drove right into the big cave on the side of the rock. Soon the storm broke over the rock in all of its fury. They could hear the roar of the storm, but they were safe. Then one of the Indians began to sing, "Rock of Ages, cleft for me, let me hide myself in Thee."

Oh, friend without Christ, the storm is coming! There is only one place of safety. It is in Jesus Christ, the Rock of Ages. Come to Him, sinner, so that you will be ready if He came tomorrow. Rededicate your life to Him, Christian, so that you will not be ashamed to meet Him.